ACADEMIC *Listening* ENCOUNTERS

HUMAN BEHAVIOR

ACADEMIC ENCOUNTERS

The *Academic Encounters* series uses a sustained-content approach to teach students the skills they need to be successful in academic courses. There are two books in the series for each content focus: an *Academic Encounters* title and an *Academic Listening Encounters* title. Please consult your catalog or contact your local sales representative for a current list of available titles.

Titles in the *Academic Encounters* series at publication:

Content Focus and Level	Components	*Academic Encounters*	*Academic Listening Encounters*
HUMAN BEHAVIOR High Intermediate to Low Advanced	Student's Book Teacher's Manual Class Audio Cassettes Class Audio CDs	ISBN 978-0-521-47658-4 ISBN 978-0-521-47660-7	ISBN 978-0-521-60620-2 ISBN 978-0-521-57820-2 ISBN 978-0-521-57819-6 ISBN 978-0-521-78357-6
LIFE IN SOCIETY Intermediate to High Intermediate	Student's Book Teacher's Manual Class Audio Cassettes Class Audio CDs	ISBN 978-0-521-66616-9 ISBN 978-0-521-66613-8	ISBN 978-0-521-75483-5 ISBN 978-0-521-75484-2 ISBN 978-0-521-75485-9 ISBN 978-0-521-75486-6
AMERICAN STUDIES Intermediate	Student's Book Teacher's Manual Class Audio CDs	ISBN 978-0-521-67369-3 ISBN 978-0-521-67370-9	ISBN 978-0-521-68432-3 ISBN 978-0-521-68434-7 ISBN 978-0-521-68433-0

2-Book Sets are available at a discounted price. Each set includes one copy of the Student's Reading Book and one copy of the Student's Listening Book.

Academic Encounters:
Human Behavior 2-Book Set
ISBN 978-0-521-89165-3

Academic Encounters:
Life in Society 2-Book Set
ISBN 978-0-521-54670-6

Academic Encounters:
American Studies 2-Book Set
ISBN 978-0-521-71013-8

ACADEMIC Listening ENCOUNTERS

HUMAN BEHAVIOR

Listening
Note Taking
Discussion

Miriam Espeseth

High Intermediate to Low Advanced

CAMBRIDGE UNIVERSITY PRESS
Cambridge, New York, Melbourne, Madrid, Cape Town, Singapore, São Paulo, Delhi

Cambridge University Press
32 Avenue of the Americas, New York, NY 10013–2473, USA

www.cambridge.org
Information on this title: www.cambridge.org/9780521606202

First published 1999
First published with Audio CD 2004
10th printing 2008

Printed in Hong Kong, China, by Golden Cup Company Limited

A catalog record for this publication is available from the British Library

ISBN 978-0-521-60620-2 Student's Book

Book design and text composition by Jill Little, Mediamark
Line drawings by Suffolk Technical Illustrators, Inc.
Photo research by Sylvia Bloch

To David

Contents

Plan of the Book

UNIT ONE Mind, Body, and Health
▶ Chapter 1: The Influence of Mind Over Body

1 Getting Started	2 American Voices	3 In Your Own Voice	4 Academic Listening and Note Taking
Skills • Reading and thinking about the topic • Examining visual material • Listening to directions	*Skills* • Predicting the content • Personalizing the topic • Listening for specific information • Comparing information from different sources • Drawing inferences *Interview Topics* • Nancy: The stress of teaching first-graders • Sam: The stress of being a police officer	*Skills* • Collecting data • Giving an oral presentation	*Skills* • Building background knowledge on the topic • Guessing vocabulary from context • Summarizing what you have heard • Sharing your cultural perspective • Comparing information from different sources *Note-Taking Skill* • Using telegraphic language *Lecture Topic* Stress and the immune system • Part One: Psychoneuro-immunology and animal studies on stress • Part Two: Human research in PNI

▶ Chapter 2: Preventing Illness

1 Getting Started	2 American Voices	3 In Your Own Voice	4 Academic Listening and Note Taking
Skills • Reading and thinking about the topic • Recalling what you already know • Listening to directions	*Skills* • Predicting the content • Restating what you have heard • Hearing versus inferring • Examining graphic material *Interview Topics* • Pat: How he started smoking, and how he finally quit • Donna, Part One: How she started smoking, and how she tried to quit • Donna, Part Two: How she stopped smoking, and how her life has changed	*Skills* • Sharing your cultural perspective • Conducting a survey	*Skills* • Building background knowledge on the topic: Vocabulary • Predicting the content • Guessing vocabulary from context • Outlining practice • Sharing your personal and cultural perspective *Note-Taking Skill* • Using symbols and abbreviations *Lecture Topic* Risk factors in cardiovascular disease • Part One: Unalterable risk factors in CVD • Part Two: Alterable risk factors in CVD

UNIT TWO Development Through Life

▶ Chapter 3: Adolescence

1 Getting Started	2 American Voices	3 In Your Own Voice	4 Academic Listening and Note Taking
Skills • Reading and thinking about the topic • Examining visual material • Recording numbers	Skills • Sharing your cultural perspective • Listening for specific information: Script writing • Listening for main ideas • Summarizing what you have heard • Drawing inferences • Looking at the cultural context Interview Topics • Jora and Eric, Part One: Freedom and responsibility • Jora and Eric, Part Two: Clothes and makeup • Jora and Eric, Part Three: Different parents, different rules	Skills • Sharing your personal perspective • Giving an oral presentation	Skills • Predicting the content • Looking for causes • Guessing vocabulary from context • Note-taking practice • Sharing your cultural perspective • Considering related information Note-Taking Skill • Using space to show organizational structure Lecture Topic Common problems of adolescents in mental health treatment • Part One: Adolescent alcohol and drug abuse • Part Two: Common problems related to school

UNIT THREE Intelligence

▶ Chapter 5: Assessing Intelligence

1 Getting Started	2 American Voices	3 In Your Own Voice	4 Academic Listening and Note Taking
Skills • Reading and thinking about the topic • Listening to directions	Skills • Personalizing the topic • Listening for specific information • Retelling • Summarizing what you have heard • Considering related information: Correlation Interview Topics • Ruth, Part One: Being a "smart kid" • Ruth, Part Two: A subject she "didn't get" • Ruth, Part Three: An incorrect label	Skills • Sharing your personal and cultural perspective • Gathering data	Skills • Predicting the content: Writing information questions • Guessing vocabulary from context • Outlining practice • Sharing your personal and cultural perspective Note-Taking Skill • Recognizing examples Lecture Topic Intelligence testing – an introduction • Part One: A history of intelligence testing • Part Two: Current approaches and some problems

▶ Chapter 4: Adulthood

1 Getting Started	2 American Voices	3 In Your Own Voice	4 Academic Listening and Note Taking
Skills • Reading and thinking about the topic • Predicting the content • Recording numbers	*Skills* • Predicting the content • Answering true/false questions • Summarizing what you have heard • Creating a chart *Interview Topics* The best age to be: • Survey, Part One: Bruce, Julie, and Ann • Survey, Part Two: Otis, Laurie, and Gene	*Skills* • Sharing your cultural perspective • Conducting a survey	*Skills* • Building background knowledge on the topic • Guessing vocabulary from context • Note-taking practice • Applying general concepts to specific data • Sharing your personal and cultural perspective *Note-Taking Skill* • Paying attention to signal words *Lecture Topic* Developmental tasks of early adulthood • Part One: Separation from parents • Part Two: The crisis of intimacy versus isolation

▶ Chapter 6: Accounting for Variations in Intelligence

1 Getting Started	2 American Voices	3 In Your Own Voice	4 Academic Listening and Note Taking
Skills • Reading and thinking about the topic • Recording numbers	*Skills* • Predicting the content • Listening for specific information • Applying general concepts to specific data • Comparing information from different sources *Interview Topics* • Dennis, Part One: Gender differences • Dennis, Part Two: Different expectations • Dennis, Part Three: Factors affecting school performance	*Skills* • Sharing your personal and cultural perspective • Giving an oral presentation	*Skills* • Predicting the content • Guessing vocabulary from context • Listening for specific information • Sharing your personal and cultural perspective • Thinking critically about the topic *Note-Taking Skill* • Recording numbers *Lecture Topic* Intelligence – nature or nurture? • Part One: Evidence for the role of nature • Part Two: Evidence for the role of nurture

UNIT FOUR Nonverbal Messages

▶ Chapter 7: **Body Language**

1 Getting Started	2 American Voices	3 In Your Own Voice	4 Academic Listening and Note Taking
Skills • Reading and thinking about the topic • Reading nonverbal cues	*Skills* • Recalling what you already know • Answering true/false questions • Restating what you have heard • Thinking critically about the topic • Considering related information *Interview Topics* • Marcos: Brazilian body language • SunRan: Korean body language • Airi: Japanese body language	*Skills* • Gathering data • Asking for clarification	*Skills* • Looking beyond the facts • Guessing vocabulary from context • Mapping • Sharing your personal and cultural perspective *Note-Taking Skill* • Mapping *Lecture Topic* Body language across cultures • Part One: Aspects of body language • Part Two: Cross-cultural misunderstandings

UNIT FIVE Interpersonal Relationships

▶ Chapter 9: **Friendship**

1 Getting Started	2 American Voices	3 In Your Own Voice	4 Academic Listening and Note Taking
Skills • Reading and thinking about the topic • Personalizing the topic • Listening for specific information	*Skills* • Recalling what you already know • Answering true/false questions • Summarizing what you have heard • Drawing inferences • Sharing your personal and cultural perspective *Interview Topics* • Catherine, Part One: Starting friendships • Catherine, Part Two: Maintaining friendships	*Skills* • Conducting a survey • Giving an oral presentation	*Skills* • Building background knowledge on the topic: Culture notes • Guessing vocabulary from context • Listening for specific information • Sharing your personal perspective • Considering related information *Note-Taking Skill* • Using morphology, context, and nonverbal cues to guess word meaning *Lecture Topic* Looking at friendship • Part One: The role of friendship in psychotherapy • Part Two: How male and female friendships differ

▶ Chapter 8: The Language of Touch, Space, and Artifacts

1 Getting Started	2 American Voices	3 In Your Own Voice	4 Academic Listening and Note Taking
Skills • Reading and thinking about the topic • Reading nonverbal cues • Listening to directions	*Skills* • Recalling what you already know • Summarizing what you have heard • Listening for specific information • Personalizing the topic • Sharing your cultural perspective • Considering related information *Interview Topics* • Marcos, SunRan, and Airi: Touch and space • Airi: Clothing	*Skills* • Gathering data • Using examples to illustrate a general point	*Skills* • Recalling what you already know • Guessing vocabulary from context • Summarizing what you have heard • Sharing your personal and cultural perspective *Note-Taking Skill* • Listening for stress and intonation *Lecture Topic* Nonverbal communication – the hidden dimension of communication • Part One: Sarcasm and proxemics • Part Two: Touch

▶ Chapter 10: Love

1 Getting Started	2 American Voices	3 In Your Own Voice	4 Academic Listening and Note Taking
Skills • Reading and thinking about the topic • Personalizing the topic • Listening for details	*Skills* • Sharing your cultural perspective • Listening for specific information • Sharing your personal and cultural perspective • Considering related information *Interview Topics* • Ann and Jim, Part One: Courtship • Ann and Jim, Part Two: Making marriage work	*Skills* • Conducting a survey • Gathering data	*Skills* • Building background knowledge on the topic • Guessing vocabulary from context • Outlining practice • Applying general concepts to specific data • Sharing your personal and cultural perspective *Note-Taking Skill* • Taking advantage of rhetorical questions *Lecture Topic* Love – what's it all about? • Part One: The matching hypothesis • Part Two: The matching hypothesis (continued) and other theories

Author's Acknowledgments

At Cambridge, thanks are due first of all to *Academic Encounters* series editor Bernard Seal for involving me in this project and providing creative grist as well as invaluable feedback throughout the long process of writing and rewriting. Thanks also to executive editor Mary Vaughn, whose clear vision and enthusiasm for the book drew me in from the start. Sue André, Janet Battiste, Jane Sturtevant, and Mary Carson have also been most helpful. Thanks to the Cambridge reviewers for their thoroughness and encouragement. My greatest debt is to the meticulous Jane Mairs. All authors should be so fortunate in their editors.

My greatest admiration and thanks also go to recording engineer Rich LePage, who assembled a cast of over forty professional actors to re-create the original interviews and lectures.

I also want to thank the ESL teachers who piloted an earlier version of the book. Their feedback was most insightful.

In Seattle, thank you to Sheila McDonell at the American Cultural Exchange for cheerfully accommodating my scheduling needs over the past two years, and allowing me to pilot the course with our ESL students. And of course, thanks to my many students who suffered through early drafts and told me what needed changing. Without their input the task would have been immeasurably more difficult and less enjoyable. Most of all, thank you to all the relatives, friends, ESL colleagues and professors who agreed to talk to me on tape for this book. Without you, there would be no book. And to Laurel Sercombe, who generously let me use her fancy tape recorder for months and months on end.

A special thanks to David Ohannesian.

Introduction

To The Instructor

About This Book

Academic Listening Encounters: Human Behavior is a content-based, listening, note-taking, and discussion book. The students who will benefit most from this book will be at the high-intermediate to low-advanced level. The topics covered were chosen for their universal appeal, and while all fall under the content umbrella of human behavior, this is a large umbrella indeed. It includes such diverse issues as who is likely to get heart disease, what it means to be an adult, and how male and female friendships differ. As students progress through the book, working on their listening, note-taking, and discussion skills, they will also acquire a basic foundation in the concepts and vocabulary of human behavior.

The complete audio program for this book, which contains the recorded material for the listening and note-taking tasks, is available on both audio CDs and audio cassettes. An audio CD of the academic lectures, which are an important part of the audio program, is included in the back of each Student's Book to provide students with additional listening practice.

About the Academic Encounters Series

This content-based series is for non-native speakers of English preparing to study in English at the college or university level and for native speakers of English who need to improve their academic skills for further study. The series consists of *Academic Encounters* books that help students improve their reading, study skills, and writing, and *Academic Listening Encounters* books that help students improve their listening, note-taking, and discussion skills. Each listening book corresponds in theme to a reading book, and each pair of theme-linked books focuses on an academic subject commonly taught in North American and other English-speaking colleges and universities. For example, *Academic Encounters: Human Behavior* and *Academic Listening Encounters: Human Behavior* both focus on psychology and human communications, and *Academic Encounters: Life in Society* and *Academic Listening Encounters: Life in Society* both focus on sociology. A reading book and a listening book with the same content focus may be used together to teach a complete four-skills course in English for Academic Purposes.

Academic Listening Encounters Listening, Note-Taking and Discussion Books

Description and Goals

Each of the five two-chapter units explores a specific topic related to the content focus of the book (in this case, human behavior). A large variety of tasks is provided for students. Many of these tasks involve listening and note taking, but others focus on critical thinking, reading, or sharing personal experiences or cultural perspectives.

The primary goal of the course is to prepare students for success in academic and everyday settings. To this end, each chapter includes both academic and informal conversational material on the same topic, accompanied by listening and note-taking tasks. A secondary goal of the course is to present relevant cultural content, with a view to promoting discussion of cultural differences and universals.

Audio Program

The heart of *Academic Listening Encounters: Human Behavior* is its authentic listening material. The audio program for each chapter includes a warm-up listening exercise designed to introduce the topic, informal interviews that explore a particular aspect of the chapter topic, and a two-part academic lecture on another aspect of the topic. Each of these three types of listening experience exposes students to a different style of discourse, while recycling vocabulary and concepts.

Tasks that involve listening to the audio material (for example, *Listening for Specific Information*, *Listening to Directions*, or *Listening for Main Ideas*) have an earphones icon 🎧 next to the title. This symbol indicates that there is material in the audio program related to the task. A second symbol 📼 indicates the exact point within the task when the audio material should be played.

The complete audio program is available on both audio CDs and audio cassettes. An audio CD of the academic lectures is included in the back of each Student's Book to provide students with additional listening practice.

Task Commentary Boxes

When a task appears for the first time, it is followed by a shaded commentary box. The material in the box explains to the student why the particular skill being introduced is important and how to practice it. A number of task types are recycled throughout the book to provide students with additional skills practice. An alphabetical index of all the tasks with the page numbers on which they occur is at the back of the book.

Note-Taking Skills

Section 4 of each chapter, *Academic Listening and Note Taking*, presents an academic note-taking skill; the presentation contains a boxed explanation of the skill, followed by a taped task providing practice with the skill. The ten note-taking tasks presented in this course were chosen to help students develop the skills they will need to be successful note takers in an academic lecture course.

Course Length

Each chapter of *Academic Listening Encounters* is divided into four sections and represents approximately 7–11 hours of classroom material (see specific suggestions for each section under *Chapter Format and Teaching Suggestions* below). Thus, with a 90-minute daily class, a teacher could complete all ten chapters in a ten-week course. For use with a shorter course, a teacher could certainly omit chapters or activities within chapters. The material could also be expanded with the use of guest speakers, debates, movies, and other authentic taped material (see the Teacher's Manual for specific suggestions).

Chapter Format and Teaching Suggestions

1 Getting Started (approximately 1 hour of class time)

This section contains a short reading task and a listening task. The reading task is designed to activate students' prior knowledge about the topic and to generate students' interest. Comprehension and discussion questions follow.

The listening task in this section is determined by the chapter content and involves one of a variety of listening skills. The task may require students to complete a graph, listen for specific information, do a matching exercise, or do something physical. This task provides skill-building practice and also gives students a listening warm-up on the chapter topic.

2 American Voices

The American Voices section contains one or more informal interviews on issues related to the chapter topic. It is divided into three subsections, described below.

Before the Interview (½ hour) This subsection contains a prelistening task that calls on students either to predict the content of the interview or to share what they already know about the topic from their personal or cultural experience. Take enough time with this task for all students to contribute. The more they invest in the topic at this point, the more they will get out of the recorded interviews.

Interviews (1– 2 hours) In this subsection students listen to the interviews. In some chapters the interviewees are native speakers of English; in others they are immigrants to the United States. The interviews are divided into two or three parts both on the audiotape and in the Student's Book to facilitate comprehension.

Each interview segment begins with a vocabulary preview, a bordered box glossing words and phrases from the interview that students may not know. These words and phrases are given in the context in which students will hear them. Read the vocabulary items out loud so that students will recognize them when they hear them pronounced in the interview. Point out that the definitions given are context-specific; some terms may have different meanings in other contexts.

After each vocabulary preview, students read either a list of questions they will be asked to answer or a partially completed summary of the interview they are about to hear. Then they listen to the recorded interview segment. After listening, they answer the questions or complete the summary. This approach allows students to demonstrate their understanding of the tape, provides a framework for listening, and teaches basic listening skills.

After the Interview (½–1 hour)   In this subsection students are given the opportunity to explore the topic more deeply through additional reading, sharing their own perspectives, drawing inferences, or thinking critically about what they have heard. Most of the tasks in this section are for pairs or small groups. Allow time for informal feedback from everyone at the close of each activity.

3   In Your Own Voice (1½–2½ hours)

Students are by now quite comfortable with the content and vocabulary of the chapter topic. The tasks in this section are designed to give them a chance to take creative control of the topic. Specific tasks are determined by the chapter content, but the following tasks are included in some form in each chapter:

- Personalizing the data: Students talk with partners or in small groups, sharing their own experiences or opinions.

- Gathering data: Students gather data by questioning one or more people, either classmates or people outside the class. This step may be done in class, as homework, or by visiting another class if one is available. If students are writing their own interview or survey questions, check their questions before they begin to gather data.

- Presenting data: Students prepare and present their data in an informal speech. Stress that this is a "practice" situation, a chance for students to get comfortable speaking to an audience in English.

4   Academic Listening and Note Taking

This section contains an authentic recorded lecture on an aspect of the chapter topic. The section is divided into three subsections, described below.

Before the Lecture (1–1½ hours)   The first task of this subsection calls on students to predict the content of the lecture, to explore what they already know about the topic, or to do a brief reading exercise designed to provide them with background information they will need to understand the lecture content. As with Before the Interview, take as much time as your students need here.

In each chapter, the lecture prelistening task is followed by the presentation of an academic note-taking skill, determined by the particular structure or language of the lecture. The skill is explained in a task commentary box, and a listening task designed to practice the skill follows. The recorded material used in the task is drawn from the lecture. Go over the information in the commentary box carefully with students before you begin the task.

Lecture (1–1½ hours)   In this subsection students hear the lecture itself. To facilitate comprehension, all lectures are divided into two parts both on the recording and in the Student's Book.

Each lecture part begins with a matching or multiple-choice vocabulary task designed to introduce vocabulary students will encounter in the lecture and help them develop their ability to guess meaning from context. Potentially unfamiliar words and phrases are given in the context in which they will be heard in the lecture. Read the words aloud so that students will hear how they are pronounced. Encourage students to recover as much meaning as possible from the context before choosing an answer.

Following the vocabulary task, students preview a comprehension task designed to provide a framework for their listening and note taking. The task may involve completing a partial summary or an outline, or answering comprehension questions. The task generally reinforces the note-taking skill taught in Before the Lecture. Students are instructed to take notes during each part of the lecture, and then to use their notes to complete the lecture comprehension task. Before they listen to each lecture part, make sure that students read over the outline, incomplete summary, or list of comprehension questions, and think about what information they will need to listen for.

After the Lecture (½–1 hour)   This subsection includes one or both of the following task types:

- Analyzing additional information: Tasks of this type allow students to deepen their understanding of the chapter topic, often by synthesizing information from the lecture and the American Voices section. Additional information related to the chapter topic is often given to students in the form of a paragraph or statistics.

- Sharing personal/cultural perspectives: Discussion questions lead students to think critically about the chapter content and to present their own views.

General Guidelines

1 Replay recorded excerpts as many times as you think will benefit the majority of students.

2 Encourage students to gain additional listening practice by listening to the chapter lectures that are on the audio CD in the back of the Student's Book. Depending on the level of the class, you may want students to listen either before or after you have played the lecture for them in class.

3 Homework assignments can include thinking and writing about discussion questions, doing Internet research, and preparing and rehearsing presentations.

4 If possible, pair students from different cultural and linguistic backgrounds.

5 Depending on your students' level of interest and time constraints,

you may want to pick and choose from the activities in After the Interview and After the Lecture. It is not necessary to do all of them.

6 To some extent, the course material builds upon itself. Skills are recycled (see the Plan of the Book) and the level of exercises increases slightly in difficulty. However, it is not necessary to do the units in order, and you can skip ones that are less appropriate for your students.

7 If you prefer to read the script of a lecture rather than play the recording, try to match the natural pace of the recorded lectures.

8 Refer to the Teacher's Manual for teaching suggestions, answer keys, the listening script, and lecture quizzes and answers.

TO THE STUDENT

Welcome to *Academic Listening Encounters: Human Behavior*. Whatever your reasons are for taking an English listening course, this book can help you. Perhaps you are planning to study at an English-language college or university. If so, the course has lectures, note-taking skills, vocabulary-building exercises, and discussion topics to prepare you for academic success. Or perhaps you want to improve your understanding of spoken American English. In each chapter you will hear North Americans talking in informal, idiomatic English on different topics, answering questions such as *What makes your marriage successful?* and *How did you quit smoking after 25 years?* If you also want speaking practice, you will find many opportunities here to discuss the topics and to present your own ideas, opinions, and cultural perspectives.

The topics presented in *Academic Listening Encounters: Human Behavior* are all related to how humans behave. If you look at the interview and lecture topics listed in the *Plan of the Book*, which follows the contents pages at the front, you will see that there is a wide range of topics, including becoming an adult, intelligence, love, and friendship. I hope that you will find the topics interesting and informative, and that this course will help you achieve your personal language goals.

Miriam Espeseth

Unit 1

Mind, Body, and Health

In this unit you will hear people discuss health and how it
can be affected by different factors, including job stress and
smoking. Chapter 1 deals with the way in which the mind affects
the body. You will hear interviews with a teacher and a police
officer, and a lecture on research concerning the link between
our mental and physical states. Chapter 2, on staying healthy,
includes interviews with two former smokers and a lecture on
how to keep your heart healthy.

1

CHAPTER 1

The Influence of Mind Over Body

1   GETTING STARTED

In this section you will examine the topic of stress, and you will listen to and perform a simple relaxation exercise.

Reading and thinking about the topic

> **I**f you have already read or thought about a topic before you hear it discussed, you will find the discussion much easier to understand.

1➤ Read the following passage.

> It seems clear that our mental attitude affects the way we feel. One good example of this concerns *stress*. Stress has become an inescapable part of modern life. There are many different causes of stress. Some are minor daily hassles, such as waiting in line or getting stuck in traffic jams. Others may be major life events, such as the death of a loved one or a divorce. There is strong evidence to show that stress affects the body's immune system, and that those who handle stress well get fewer and less serious illnesses. People who are under a great deal of stress need to learn to cope with and relieve their stress in order to stay healthy.

2➤ Answer the following questions according to the information in the passage.

  1 What major and minor life events can cause stress?

  2 How does stress cause illness?

  3 What should someone under stress learn to do?

3➤ Discuss your own experiences and opinions with a partner.

   1 Can you think of some other sources of stress not mentioned in the passage?

   2 Do you believe that people under stress are more likely to get sick than those who are not under stress?

   3 Can you think of some ways to relieve stress?

Examining visual material

> **A**lways pay attention to visual material. The pictures, photographs, and charts in books will help you understand what you are reading, and watching people's faces and gestures as they speak will help you understand what you are hearing.

Look at the photograph to the right and discuss the following with a group of classmates.

   1 What do you think the person in this photograph is listening to?

   2 If you were the person in this photograph, what would you be listening to?

   3 What kinds of sounds do you find relaxing?

🎧 Listening to directions

> **M**any everyday listening activities do not require you to speak, write, or remember information for later use. Instead, you must simply follow directions.

1➤ Listen to the tape and follow the speaker's directions. 📼

2➤ Write a few short sentences to describe how your body feels.

   I feel _____

   _____

   _____

3➤ Read what you wrote to a small group of classmates. Listen to what they wrote. Then answer the following questions in your small group.

   1 Have you ever done a relaxation exercise like the one you just did?

   2 What are the benefits of this kind of exercise?

2   AMERICAN VOICES: Nancy and Sam

In this section you will hear interviews with two people with very stressful jobs: Nancy, a first-grade teacher, and Sam, an officer with the Los Angeles Police Department (LAPD).

BEFORE THE INTERVIEWS

Predicting the content

> In any listening context, thinking about and trying to predict what you will hear can greatly increase your comprehension.

1▶ Think about why it might be stressful to be an elementary school teacher or a police officer. Write your ideas in the boxes.

Teaching children is stressful because:	Being a police officer is stressful because:

2▶ Share ideas as a class. If you hear new ideas, add them to your lists.

INTERVIEW WITH NANCY: The stress of teaching first-graders

Here are some words and expressions used in the interview, printed in **boldface** and given in the context in which you will hear them. They are followed by definitions.

*trying to teach a new **concept**:* idea
*there's a **disruptive** child:* causing problems; behaving badly
*It pulls everyone **off track**:* away from the work that is being done
*things that are in the **curriculum**:* material that must be taught at a specific grade level
***How** does the stress **manifest itself**?:* what are the signs or symptoms
***Fatigue!**:* being tired
*I have to **keep my temper** in the classroom:* not become angry
*You're **more susceptible to illness**:* get sick more easily and more often
*It weakens your **immune system**:* body's defenses against disease

🎧 Personalizing the topic

> **T**hinking about your own experiences and ideas related to a topic can help you understand and remember the information that you hear.

1➤ How stressed are you? The following list is from a medical pamphlet on stress. It describes frequent signs of too much stress. Read the list. Write your initials in front of any symptoms you are currently experiencing.

FREQUENT SIGNS OF TOO MUCH STRESS	
_____ Problems eating or sleeping	❏
_____ Increased boredom and great fatigue	❏
_____ Problems making decisions	❏
_____ Increased feelings of anger when small things go wrong	❏
_____ Frequent headaches, backaches, muscle aches, stomach problems	❏
_____ Frequent colds and infections	❏

2➤ Now listen. Place a check (✓) in the box next to the stress symptoms that Nancy has. 📼

3➤ Compare answers as a class.

🎧 Listening for specific information

> **L**istening for specific information is a useful skill to practice for almost every kind of listening task. Whether we are at school, on the phone, or shopping, we usually listen for specific information, and not for every word.

1➤ Read the following questions. Answer as many as you can from your first listening.

1 How long has Nancy taught, and at what levels?

2 Why is teaching more stressful than other jobs, in her opinion?

3 Nancy says that she is sometimes impatient with her own child. Why?

4 What two reasons does Nancy give to explain why she is often sick?

5 What are two things that Nancy does to relieve her stress?

Nancy with her students

2▶ Now listen to the interview again. Try to listen for the specific information that you need in order to complete your answers in Step 1. Then finish your answers. 📼

3▶ Compare answers with a partner.

INTERVIEW WITH SAM: The stress of being a police officer

> Here are some words and expressions from the interview, printed in **boldface** and given in the context in which you will hear them. They are followed by definitions.
>
> *different types of* **assignments**: specific jobs within the police department
> ***patrol***: an assignment in which a police officer walks, bicycles, or drives around a certain neighborhood
> *a **traffic violation***: something illegal that is done by a driver
> *a **routine** stop*: regular; not special or unusual
> ***the force***: the police force; the police as a group
> ***ulcers***: holes in the lining of the stomach that are made worse by stress
> *It's **documented***: shown to be true by research; proven
> *keep a relationship* ***at its peak***: in very good condition; very healthy

🎧 *Listening for specific information*

1▶ Read the following questions before you listen to the interview with Sam.

1 How long has Sam been a police officer?

2 What does Sam consider the most stressful assignment, and why?

3 What does Sam say about illness on the police force?

4 What programs does the LAPD have to help officers cope with job stress?

5 How does Sam deal with his stress?

2▶ Now listen to the interview. Try to listen specifically for answers to the questions in Step 1. Write short answers. 📼

Sam

3▶ Compare answers with a partner and then with the class. Listen again if you need to.

AFTER THE INTERVIEWS
Comparing information from different sources

> Whether you are reading or listening, one way to deepen your understanding of a topic is to compare information from different sources.

1➤ Read the following advice from the same medical pamphlet on stress. (See page 5.)

HOW TO DEAL WITH STRESS
_____ Become part of a support system: Let your friends or co-workers help you when you are under too much stress, and try to help them, too.
_____ Think positively: Don't worry about things that may not happen. If you do, your mind will send negative signals to your body.
_____ Anticipate stressful situations: If you know that you will be in a stressful situation, plan what you will do and say.
_____ Take care of your health: Exercise regularly, eat well, get enough sleep.
_____ Make time for yourself: Every day, take some time – even if it's just a few minutes – to be alone, to relax, to do something just for yourself.

2➤ Which of the suggestions does Nancy follow? Write _N_ next to these. Which ones does Sam or the LAPD follow? Write _S_ next to these. Then compare answers with a partner. Discuss any differences.

Drawing inferences

> When you listen to people speak, you must not only think about what they tell you directly but also be aware of what they communicate indirectly. Drawing inferences, or gathering information beyond what a speaker actually says, is a critical aspect of listening.

1➤ Read the following statements about the interviews that you heard. Write whether you agree (_A_) or disagree (_D_) with each statement.

_____ 1 Nancy is probably in her early thirties.

_____ 2 She takes her job very seriously.

_____ 3 She doesn't teach during the summer.

_____ 4 She enjoys her work as a teacher.

_____ 5 Sam is probably in his forties.

_____ 6 Patrol officers probably experience less illness than supervisors.

_____ 7 Sam likes being a police officer.

2➤ Work with a partner. Check to see if you drew the same inferences. Explain why you wrote what you did. You may disagree about some of the statements.

3 IN YOUR OWN VOICE

In this section you will do some research of your own on work and stress.

Collecting data

> **Y**ou can learn more about a topic by collecting your own data. One easy way is by asking other people for their opinions.

1➤ Work with a partner. Make a list of ten jobs that you think are very stressful. Discuss why you think so.

2➤ Share your lists as a class. Discuss your choices and give reasons for them. Then vote and create a class list of the ten most stressful jobs.

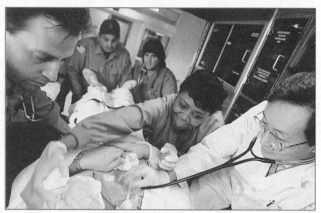

Emergency room staff and ambulance workers

Giving an oral presentation

> **Y**ou will sometimes be called on in academic courses to give oral presentations in class. Here are some guidelines to keep in mind:
> - Plan what you want to say, but do not write it out and memorize it. Rather, make notes on 3-x 5-inch note cards.
> - Using your notes, practice giving your speech in front of a mirror or for a friend.
> - When you give your presentation in class, speak slowly and clearly, and look at your audience.

1➤ Work with a partner. Tell each other about the stress of your present job – being an English student. Answer the following questions, and give details and examples.

> **Causes:** What is stressful about being a student? Give specific examples.
>
> **Effects:** What are the symptoms of your stress (e.g., health effects)?
>
> **Solutions:** How do you cope with your stress?

2➤ Using the information that you shared with your partner, give a short speech to the class about the stress of being a student and how to cope with it. Add other information if you like.

4   ACADEMIC LISTENING AND NOTE TAKING: Stress and the immune system

In this section you will hear and take notes on a two-part lecture given by Ellen Cash, a professor of psychology. The title of the lecture is *Stress and the Immune System*. Professor Cash will present research supporting the idea that the mind can affect the body.

BEFORE THE LECTURE

Building background knowledge on the topic

> When you attend a lecture, you almost always know beforehand what topic it will cover. It is a good idea to do some background reading on the topic first and to look up any unfamiliar words or ideas.

1➤ Read the following description of the lecture from Professor Cash's course syllabus.

> *Week 4 Lecture: Stress and the immune system*
> • psychosomatic disorders
> • animal and human research
> • classical conditioning (stimulus-response)
> • implications for health care

2➤ According to this lecture description, Professor Cash will talk about *classical conditioning* in her lecture. Let's do some background reading on conditioning.

> *Classical conditioning* was first identified by Ivan Pavlov in the salivation reflex of dogs. Salivation is an unconditioned response to food, which is an unconditioned stimulus. Pavlov showed that dogs could be conditioned over time to salivate merely to the sound of a bell (a conditioned stimulus), if the bell was rung at the same time that food was presented on a series of occasions. When this happens, learning is said to have occurred because salivation has been conditioned to a new stimulus (the bell) that did not cause it at first.

3➤ Work with a partner. Summarize Pavlov's experiment by completing the following with terms from the reading.

Food (*an* _____ *stimulus*) naturally makes a dog salivate (*an* _____ *response*). If we always ring a bell (*a* _____ *stimulus*) as we feed the dog, after a while the dog will salivate when it hears the bell even without the food (*a* _____ *response*).

4➤ With a small group, discuss the other terms mentioned in the lecture description in Step 1. Look up any terms you do not understand in a dictionary, or ask your teacher for help.

🎧 Note taking: Using telegraphic language

Lecture note taking is a complex skill, and developing it requires a great deal of practice. One of the first things you have to learn is that when you listen to a lecture, it is not possible to write down everything. And even if you could, doing so would not be a good idea! Many lecturers repeat themselves, go off the topic, and tell unrelated personal stories.

Good note takers can recognize what is important and what is not. They are able to get the important information down on paper in as few words as possible, using abbreviations and symbols. At the same time, they organize the information on the page to show what is a main point and what is a detail or example. These are all important skills to develop, and as you study this book, you will practice each of them.

The first step, however, is to learn to listen to several sentences of a lecture and quickly summarize the information in your own words. You must also train yourself to leave out unnecessary words, such as articles, prepositions, relative pronouns, the verb *to be*, and other linking verbs. In other words, you need to learn to use what is called *telegraphic language*.

1➤ Read the following sentences. Each one summarizes an excerpt from the lecture on stress and the immune system, and presents an important point in the lecture.

_____ *a* There is research to support the idea that stress hurts the immune system.

_____

_____ *b* More doctors (*etc.*) now agree that learning to relax sometimes cures better than drugs.

_____

_____ *c* Many common health problems may begin in the mind (*psychosomatic*).

_____

_____ *d* Research shows that when sick people feel helpless, their health gets worse.

_____

2➤ Now listen to the four short excerpts and match them with the correct summaries in Step 1. Write the numbers in the blanks. 📼

3➤ Using the blank lines in Step 1, rewrite the sentences in telegraphic language, as if they were lecture notes – that is, leave out words that are not needed. Be sure to leave enough information so that you can understand your notes. Here is an example of what to do.

> The immune system recognizes foreign invaders and kills them.
>
> *immune system – finds and kills invaders*

4➤ Compare matches and notes as a class.

LECTURE, Part One: Psychoneuroimmunology and animal studies on stress

Guessing vocabulary from context

> **W**hen you hear or read words that you do not know, pay attention to the surrounding words for clues to their meaning.

1➤ The following items contain some important vocabulary from Part One of the lecture. Each of the vocabulary words is printed in **boldface**, in the context in which it occurs, together with three possible definitions. Use the context to help you choose the best definition for each word. Then check your guesses in a dictionary.

1 Stress has real **implications** in terms of what it can do to the body.
   a consequences   *b* choices   *c* experiences

2 **psychosomatic** disorders, where a physical symptom is caused by a psychological problem
   a affecting the mind   *b* caused by the mind   *c* very dangerous

3 to recognize foreign **invaders**, things that come into the body
   a animals   *b* attackers   *c* medicines

4 to **inactivate** the invaders and remove them
   a eat   *b* cause not to work   *c* get rid of

5 The immune system is **compromised**, damaged, by certain stressors.
   a improved   *b* assisted   *c* hurt

6 He was able to **condition** the rats' immune systems to malfunction.
   a teach   *b* assist   *c* punish

7 If we can condition immune systems to **malfunction**, then it makes sense that we could also condition them to get better.
   a speed up   *b* work harder   *c* not work correctly

2➤ Compare answers with a partner. Ask your teacher for help if you need to.

🎧 *Summarizing what you have heard*

Summarizing involves reducing a long piece of text (written or spoken) to a few clear sentences, written in your own words. With something as long as a lecture, summarizing is the last of several steps. During the lecture, take notes in whatever way works best for you. After the lecture, go over your notes, reconstruct what you have heard, and decide which material is important. Now you are ready to write your summary. Summarizing is an essential skill because it shows that you have understood what is important in a reading or a lecture. It also provides you with a record for your own review purposes.

1➤ The following is an incomplete summary of Part One of the lecture. Read the summary and think about what kinds of words or phrases might go in the blanks. Do not write anything yet.

STRESS AND THE IMMUNE SYSTEM, Part One

There is a lot of evidence to support the idea that our minds can affect our _____ . Many of the health problems that people suffer, such as headaches, _____ , and _____ , may be related to psychosomatic disorders – that is, they may be caused by the _____ .

The new field of *psychoneuroimmunology* (PNI) studies the way in which our minds can affect our _____ . In a healthy person, the immune system protects the body against _____ . Animal and human research has shown that stress – especially uncontrollable stress – can hurt the immune system.

Robert Ader did an important study with rats in which he learned, quite by accident, that the rats' _____ could be conditioned to _____ . This was an exciting discovery for science: if the immune system can be taught to _____ , that probably means that it can also learn to _____ .

2➤ Now listen to Part One of the lecture. Take notes on your own paper. Remember, it is not necessary to write down everything that you hear. Use the summary in the box as a guide to help you listen for the important points. Use telegraphic language in your notes to save time. 📼

3➤ Use your notes to complete the summary in the box.

4➤ Compare summaries with a partner. Do you have similar answers? You do not have to have exactly the same words because summaries are in your *own* words.

LECTURE, Part Two: Human research in PNI

Guessing vocabulary from context

1► The following items contain some important vocabulary from Part Two of the lecture. Use the context to help you choose the best definitions. Then check your guesses in a dictionary.

1 when people are under great stress, for example, **accountants** before tax time
   a employers   *b* people who type reports   *c* people who figure taxes

2 so here the mental stress is acting as a conditioned **stimulus**
   a something that makes us react   *b* something helpful   *c* something negative

3 elderly people in **nursing homes**
   a homes for sick and older people   *b* hotels   *c* homes for nurses

4 the ones who felt in control **tended to be** healthier
   a were always   *b* were never   *c* were usually

5 Relaxation techniques can be very effective – more effective than **medication.**
   a drugs   *b* medical care   *c* hospitalization

2► Compare answers with a partner. Ask your teacher for help if necessary.

🎧 Summarizing what you have heard

1► Read the following incomplete summary of Part Two of the lecture. Be sure that you understand all the words. Think about what information you will need to fill in the blanks.

STRESS AND THE IMMUNE SYSTEM, Part Two

There are also _____ studies to support the idea that the mind can _____ . Just *thinking* about stressful situations can suppress the _____ . This has been seen in studies on accountants before tax time, and on _____ before _____ . Also, if people feel out of control, this can compromise their _____ . Studies show that people in nursing homes who didn't choose to _____ are more likely to get sick than people who _____ .

   People in the _____ field are becoming more interested in PNI. We see this, for example, in the treatment of headaches and _____ . More doctors and nurses today are teaching their _____ to control these problems by using _____ rather than medication.

2► Now listen to Part Two of the lecture. Take notes on your own paper. Remember to use telegraphic language. 📼

3➤ Use your notes to complete the summary in the box.

4➤ Compare summaries with a partner. Remember, your summaries do not have to be exactly the same.

AFTER THE LECTURE

Sharing your cultural perspective

> An issue becomes more interesting if you share your own cultural perspective on it and hear the perspective of people from other cultures.

Discuss the following questions with one or two classmates.

1 For centuries, Western medicine has treated the body and paid almost no attention to the mind. As Professor Cash stated, health-care professionals are now starting to understand that the mind plays a powerful role in the health of the body. How does traditional medical practice in your culture view the connection between the mind and the body?

2 How does this view affect the way doctors and other health-care givers treat patients?

Comparing information from different sources

Read the following text and discuss the questions as a class.

> The following research findings were reported in the *U.C. Berkeley Wellness Newsletter*. Various studies on stress and immunology found that:
>
> • During times of great stress – for example, exams – students' immune cells became less active, and their resistance to disease decreased.
>
> • "Highly stressed" people caught colds more easily than other people.
>
> • People who had recently lost a husband or wife had higher rates of illness and death than others.
>
> • Patients with cancer lived longer if they had a "fighting spirit," and cancer patients who felt depressed about their illness died sooner.

1 Compare this information with what you heard in the lecture. Is it consistent with what Professor Cash described?

2 Do you have any personal experience that supports these findings? For example, have you (or someone you know) ever gotten sick during a stressful time?

CHAPTER 2

Preventing Illness

1   GETTING STARTED

In this section you are going to discuss what people do to stay healthy, and you will perform a small experiment involving your muscles and heart rate.

Reading and thinking about the topic

1► Read the following passage.

> There is a common saying: "If you've got your health, you've got everything." To some extent, good health is a function of genetics, but there are actions we can take to help prevent illness. In recent years, Americans have become more interested in their health. For example, as the medical evidence against the use of tobacco grows, fewer people are smoking. Another sign of our concern with health is the current exercise boom. Recently, medical research has shown a connection between aerobic exercise and cardiovascular health. As a result, Americans of all ages are taking up jogging, walking, or other forms of aerobic exercise.

2► Answer the following questions.

  1 What does, "If you've got your health, you've got everything," mean?
  2 What are two things that Americans are doing to stay well and fit?
  3 What is motivating them to do these things?

3► Discuss your own experiences and opinions with a partner.

  1 Do you agree with the saying quoted in the passage? Explain your answer.
  2 Are there some things you do to stay healthy that are not mentioned in the passage?

Recalling what you already know

> **R**ecalling what you already know about a topic beforehand will make a discussion of that topic easier for you to follow.

Take turns asking and answering the following questions with a partner. Make your answers as clear and as simple as you can.

1 What does the term *heart rate* mean?

2 How can you measure your heart rate?

3 What happens when your heart beats?

4 Your heart rate does not stay the same all the time. How and why does it change?

Listening to directions

1► Listen to the tape and follow the speaker's directions.

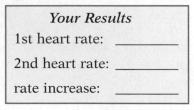

Your Results

1st heart rate: _____

2nd heart rate: _____

rate increase: _____

2► Discuss the following questions with a small group of classmates.

1 Were your heart rates faster the second time that you measured them? If so, explain why as clearly and as completely as you can.

2 What are some other activities, situations, or conditions that can cause heart rate to increase?

3 In general, which indicates a healthier heart when you are at rest: a fast rate or a slow rate?

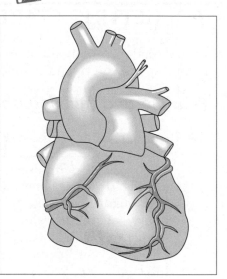

The human heart

3► Figure out class averages for the first and second heart rates and the average increase. Record them.

Class Results

1st average: _____

2nd average: _____

average increase: _____

2 AMERICAN VOICES: Pat and Donna

In this section you will hear interviews with two ex-smokers, Pat and Donna. They will talk about how they began smoking, how long they smoked, and how they managed to quit.

BEFORE THE INTERVIEWS

Predicting the content

1➤ Answer the following questions with a partner.

1 Why do people start smoking?

2 Why is it so difficult to quit smoking?

3 What are some of the methods that people use to stop smoking?

4 What are some of the benefits of giving up smoking?

2➤ Share answers as a class.

THE FAR SIDE   By GARY LARSON

© 1982 FarWorks Inc. All Rights Reserved

Primitive peer pressure

INTERVIEW WITH PAT: How he started smoking, and how he finally quit

Here are some words and expressions used in the interview, printed in **boldface** and given in the context in which you will hear them. They are followed by definitions.

*I smoked **heavily**:* a lot; a great deal

*I **switched** to a pipe:* changed

*Smoking was **cool**:* good; socially desirable (informal)

***peer pressure**:* feeling the need to do something because one's friends are doing it

*It **never did any good**:* had no effect; was not helpful

*just [used] **will power**:* made a promise to do something and tried to keep it

*I wasn't **hooked** anymore:* addicted (as to a drug) (informal)

*You've never **been tempted** to start smoking again:* wanted to do something badly but haven't actually done it

🎧 Restating what you have heard

> As a student, you will often need to restate information that you have heard or read. This task requires you to grasp the message completely enough to paraphrase it – that is, to express the same ideas with different words. When you paraphrase, you are showing not only that you remember what you heard or read but also that you understand it.

1➤ Read the following incomplete restatement before you listen to the interview with Pat. Think about what kind of information you will need to fill in the blanks.

Pat

> Pat was _____ or _____ years old when he started smoking. He smoked about _____ cigarettes a day. Pat smoked cigarettes, and later a _____, for a total of _____ years. He tried to _____ many times. In high school, he gave up cigarettes while he was on the _____ team, but he _____ again after the _____ game. Pat finally quit smoking in _____ because he had a _____ . He has _____ been tempted to _____ again.

2➤ Now listen to the interview with Pat. Try to listen for the information that you will need to complete the restatement in Step 1. 📼

3➤ Fill in the blanks in the box. Then compare restatements with a partner. They do not have to be exactly the same. Listen again if you need to.

INTERVIEW WITH DONNA, Part One: How she started smoking, and how she tried to quit

Here are some words and expressions used in Part One of the interview.

A lot of my friends **would** *get together after school:* did as a habit; used to

in South America as an **exchange student***:* one who attends school for a while in another country, living with a family

We **hung out** *in coffee shops:* spent time; relaxed (slang)

and smoked **Gauloises***:* a French brand of unfiltered cigarettes

chronic bronchitis*:* long-term or repeated inflammation of the airways leading to the lungs

initially*:* at first

I just **went cold turkey***:* stopped using a drug suddenly and completely

I **cut back** *so I was hardly smoking at all:* reduced; decreased

🎧 *Restating what you have heard*

1► Read the following incomplete restatement before you listen to Part One of the interview with Donna. Think about what kind of information you will need to complete it.

Donna started smoking at about age _____ or _____ . She and her friends would get together after _____ . They would eat _____ and smoke cigarettes. After a while, Donna was smoking a _____ a day. She kept smoking for _____ more years.

Donna studied in South _____, and later she taught in _____. In both places, smoking was _____ common than in the United States. People smoked in public places, for example, in _____ and _____. When Donna returned to the United States, she went to _____ school. She and her friends would drink _____ and smoke _____.

But Donna wasn't feeling very _____. She had chronic bronchitis. She tried to quit many times but could not. Later, when she was married and _____, she nearly stopped. But as soon as her _____ was born, she _____ .

Donna

2► Now listen to Part One of the interview with Donna. Try to listen for the information that you will need to complete the restatement in Step 1.

3► Fill in the blanks in the box. Then compare paragraphs with a partner. They do not have to be exactly the same. Listen again if you need to.

INTERVIEW WITH DONNA, Part Two: How she stopped smoking, and how her life has changed

Here are some words and expressions used in Part Two of the interview.

*This woman **hypnotized** him:* put someone into a sleeplike state, then gave him or her suggestions

*I had four **treatments**:* appointments with someone who gives a service (e.g., a hypnotist or a physical therapist)

*completely lost the **urge** to smoke:* desire; temptation

*celebrate our **anniversary**:* the date every year on which something important happened

*I've **kept** doing that:* continued

🎧 Restating what you have heard

1▶ The following is an incomplete restatement of Part Two of the interview with Donna. Read it and think about what kind of information you will need to complete it.

> Finally, a friend of Donna's recommended a hypnotherapist. This friend had been a very heavy smoker – _____ packs a _____ – but the hypnotherapist had helped him _____ . Donna decided to go and get hypnotized herself, and the treatment _____!
>
> Donna believes that she was able to _____ this time because _____ . Donna's _____ was _____ when she quit because he had always _____ about her _____ . Soon, Donna started to feel _____ physically. She noticed that she had a lot more _____ , and she could _____ things again. Also, food started to _____ to her. A final advantage was _____.
>
> After she quit, Donna decided to _____ all of the _____ that she had been spending on _____ and buy _____ gifts for herself and her son. Exactly one _____ after she quit smoking, she bought them _____ . She has continued _____ _____ .

2▶ Now listen to Part Two of the interview with Donna. Try to listen for the information that you will need to complete the restatement in Step 1. 📼

3▶ Fill in the blanks in the box. Then compare restatements with a partner. They do not have to be the same. Listen again if you need to.

Donna on her bicycle

AFTER THE INTERVIEWS

Hearing versus inferring

When we listen to someone speak, we draw inferences beyond their actual words. While inferences are an essential part of any message, it is important to be aware of the difference between what we actually hear and what we guess at.

1➤ Complete the accompanying chart. Under *Pat* and *Donna*, write the letters of all the answers that fit each one, based on what you actually heard in their interviews. If you did not actually hear a particular answer, but think that it is true, write the letter followed by *I* (inference).

	Pat	Donna
Why did you start smoking?		
a peer pressure	_____	_____
b It was "cool."	_____	_____
c cigarette advertising	_____	_____
How long did you smoke?		
a 10–15 years	_____	_____
b 16–20 years	_____	_____
c 21–30 years	_____	_____
What physical problems did smoking cause?		
a heart disease	_____	_____
b bronchitis	_____	_____
c low energy	_____	_____
d inability to taste and smell	_____	_____
What methods(s) did you use to try to quit?		
a will power	_____	_____
b candy	_____	_____
c hypnosis	_____	_____
Do you ever feel like smoking now?		
a Yes	_____	_____
b No	_____	_____

2➤ Compare charts with a partner. Discuss and explain your answers. Your guesses may not be exactly the same.

Examining graphic material

> A lot of the information that you encounter both in and out of the classroom is presented in graphic form, so it's important to be able to read and analyze graphs and charts.

Study the accompanying graph and answer the questions with a group of classmates.

1 Which country has the greatest percentage of smokers (the average of men and women combined)?

2 Which has the lowest percentage of smokers (the average of men and women combined)?

3 What differences do you see concerning smoking and gender?

4 Is there anything in the graph that you find surprising?

5 If your country is not included here, can you guess where it would fall on the graph?

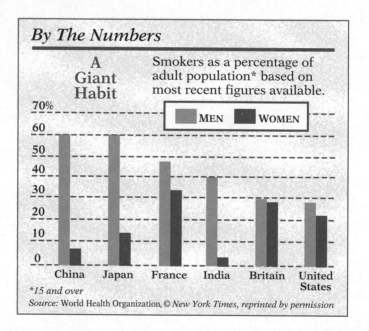

By The Numbers

A Giant Habit

Smokers as a percentage of adult population* based on most recent figures available.

MEN   WOMEN

70%
60
50
40
30
20
10
0

China   Japan   France   India   Britain   United States

*15 and over

Source: World Health Organization, © New York Times, reprinted by permission

3   IN YOUR OWN VOICE

In this section you will discuss and do research on smoking and other habits that affect your health.

Sharing your cultural perspective

Discuss the following questions with one or two classmates – with those who are from other cultures, if possible.

1 Pat's parents knew that he smoked, but Donna kept her smoking a secret from her parents as long as she could. Can you think of any reasons for this difference? In your culture, is it more acceptable for men to smoke than it is for women?

2 Pat and Donna both started smoking fairly young. In the United States, it is illegal for children under eighteen to buy cigarettes. How do you think they got their cigarettes? In your country, do many teenagers smoke? Can they buy cigarettes legally?

3 A recent study reported that people who work in restaurants where there is a great deal of smoke from customers (called "second-hand smoke") may be 50 percent more likely to get lung cancer than the average person. Is smoking controlled or prohibited in restaurants or other public places in your country? Do you think it should be?

Conducting a survey

Conducting a survey is a simple way to gather and compare data about a large number of people. The following guidelines will help you design a successful survey.

- Decide what topic you would like to research in your survey. Be sure that your topic is not too broad. For example, *second-hand smoke* is a good choice, while *health* is much too general.
- Plan to interview at least twenty people. Interview people who will be familiar with your topic.
- Make sure that your questions are clear and easy to answer. See if a classmate or a friend can answer them!
- Think of all the possible answers you may get in response to each question, and make sure that your questions will produce the information you are seeking. Avoid questions with obvious answers like "Do you like to be healthy?" because everyone will say yes, and you won't learn anything.
- A survey involves interviewing many people, so make sure that your questions will produce short, specific answers. Answers to multiple-choice and yes/no questions are the easiest to analyze.

Do the following activity alone or with a partner.

1➤ Think of an interesting topic related to health or habits, such as attitudes toward smoking, exercise, or diet. Choose a topic that interests you.

2➤ Write three or four questions about your topic. Write them in a multiple-choice format. Here is an example.

How many hours a week do you exercise?

(a) 0 – 1

(b) 2 – 5

(c) 6 – 10

(d) more than 10

3➤ Survey at least twenty people. Make a checklist like this one to record their answers.

				Question 1				Question 2				Question 3	
	M	F	natl.	a	b	c	d	a	b	c	d	Y	N
1	✓		Japanese		✓					✓		✓	
2		✓	Korean	✓					✓				✓
3		✓	Mexican			✓		✓					✓
4													
etc.													

4➤ Finally, analyze your data. Add up responses and see if there are major differences between males and females or among different nationalities. Express the results in percentages and give a brief report to your class.

Sixty percent of the men I surveyed smoke cigarettes, but only 25% of the women do.

4 ACADEMIC LISTENING AND NOTE TAKING: Risk factors in cardiovascular disease

In this section you will hear and take notes on a two-part lecture given by Kristine Moore, a registered nurse and clinical nursing specialist. The title of the lecture is *Risk Factors in Cardiovascular Disease*. Ms. Moore will discuss what conditions and habits make a person more likely to have cardiovascular problems.

BEFORE THE LECTURE

Building background knowledge on the topic: Vocabulary

> If the title of a lecture has a technical term in it, look it up beforehand in a good English–English dictionary. If the definition contains other terms you are not familiar with, look these up as well. The dictionary entries for these other terms may lead you to look up still more new words. The new vocabulary that you learn in this way will help you understand the lecture better.

1➤ The lecture that you will hear deals with *cardiovascular disease*. To get a better understanding of what cardiovascular disease is, read the dictionary entries in the box.

---

cardio- *(prefix)* Relating to the heart.

cardiovascular *(adjective)* Involving, or relating to, the heart and the blood vessels.

blood vessel *(noun)* An elastic canal shaped like a tube that carries blood to or from the heart, such as an artery or a vein.

artery *(noun, Anatomy)* Any of a branching system of tubular vessels that carry blood away from the heart.

vein *(noun, Anatomy)* Any of a branching system of tubular vessels that carry blood toward the heart.

2➤ Answer these questions with a partner.
  1 What do you think "vascular" means?
  2 What is the difference between an artery and a vein?

Predicting the content

> Sometimes you can predict a great deal from the title of a lecture. Doing this will usually increase your listening comprehension.

1► Discuss the following questions with two classmates.

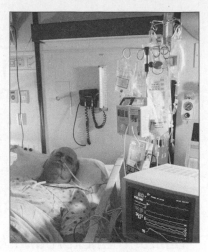

1 The lecture title is *Risk Factors in Cardiovascular Disease*. What are some things that can go wrong with the cardiovascular system? What serious health problems can occur as a result?

2 What risk factors do you think the lecturer will present? Try to name some habits or conditions (*risk factors*) that can lead to cardiovascular disease.

2► As a class, compile your predictions on the board.

🎧 Note taking: Using symbols and abbreviations

When you take notes during a lecture, you have to write down a lot of information very quickly. Rather than writing every word in full, get into the habit of using *symbols* and *abbreviations*. Some common examples of each are listed here in **boldface** with their meanings in parentheses ( ).

Symbols   Here are some symbols commonly used in English. Many of them come from the field of mathematics.

& (and)	**=** (is the same as, means)
@ (at)	**≠** (is different from, doesn't mean)
< (is less than)	**∴** (therefore)
> (is greater than)	

Abbreviations   Good note takers also commonly abbreviate (shorten) long or frequently occurring words. Some abbreviations are standard: Any English speaker will know what they mean. Here are some standard abbreviations. Notice that some are based on Latin words.

abt. (about)	**e.g.** (for example, from the Latin *exempli gratia*)
gov't (government)	**A.M.** (before noon, from the Latin *ante meridiem*)
hosp. (hospital)	**P.M.** (after noon, from the Latin *post meridiem*)
MD (medical doctor)	**intell.** (intelligence, intelligent)
med. (medicine, medical)	**IQ** (intelligence quotient)
TV (television)	**admin.** (administration, administrative)
w/ (with)	

You may want to adopt some of these symbols and abbreviations, and you will probably also want to invent some of your own, depending on the content of the lecture you are hearing. When you invent symbols and abbreviations, it is important to review your notes as soon as possible after the lecture, while their meanings are still fresh in your mind.

1➤ Study the symbols and abbreviations on the left. Match them with their meanings on the right. Notice the way in which each of the abbreviations was created.

_____	*1* CVD	*a*	is; means; is the same as
_____	*2* PVD	*b*	with
_____	*3* →	*c*	artery; arteries
_____	*4* e.g.	*d*	reduce; lower; decrease
_____	*5* ↗	*e*	increase; higher
_____	*6* ↘	*f*	high blood pressure
_____	*7* pers.	*g*	at least; greater than or equal to
_____	*8* HBP	*h*	female; women
_____	*9* =	*i*	male; men
_____	*10* art.	*j*	causes; results in
_____	*11* ♂	*k*	for example
_____	*12* ♀	*l*	peripheral vascular disease
_____	*13* ❤	*m*	cardiovascular disease
_____	*14* w/	*n*	heart
_____	*15* ≥	*o*	person; personality

2➤ Compare matches with a partner.

3➤ Now listen to four excerpts from the lecture. Take notes as you listen, using symbols and abbreviations. The ones mentioned above are only suggestions; you may use different ones if you prefer. Remember also to leave out unnecessary words, as you did in the task *Note taking: Using telegraphic language*, in Chapter 1, Section 4.

4➤ Use your notes to tell a partner what you heard. Did you hear the same things?

LECTURE, Part One: Unalterable risk factors in CVD

Guessing vocabulary from context

1➤ The items on the next page contain some important vocabulary from Part One of the lecture. Each of the terms is in **boldface** in the context in which you will hear it.

Work with a partner. Take turns explaining what you think each term means, based on its context. In some cases you may be able to give only a general idea, but this can still contribute to your overall understanding of the term. For example, is it a noun or an adjective? Does it mean something good or something bad?

_____ 1 In a **stroke**, there is blocking of the arteries that feed the brain.

_____ 2 **peripheral** vascular disease, which is also known as clots to the legs

_____ 3 In **clots** to the legs, there is blocking of one or more arteries.

_____ 4 a loss of **elasticity**, so the arteries aren't as flexible

_____ 5 **partial** or complete blocking of the arteries

_____ 6 **estrogen**, a hormone that is made in women's bodies

_____ 7 a hormone which is made in women's bodies up until **menopause**

_____ 8 People with **diabetes** have a higher rate of cardiovascular disease.

_____ 9 certain amounts of fats that our bodies use **metabolically**

_____ 10 **cholesterol**, and some of these other fat-containing chemicals

_____ 11 And this is to some extent **hereditary** – usually because of family history.

2➤ Match the vocabulary terms in Step 1 with their definitions by writing the letters in the blanks. Note that the definitions reflect the way in which the terms are used in the lecture; some of these terms can have different meanings in other contexts.

_a_ not complete; in part
_b_ a chemical produced in females
_c_ acting as fuel to make the body work
_d_ waxlike material produced by the body and necessary for its functioning
_e_ the time of life after which women can no longer have children
_f_ inherited; passed from one generation to the next
_g_ flexibility; ability to bend and stretch
_h_ balls of fat that block blood flow in arteries
_i_ disease in which the body cannot make insulin, which controls blood sugar
_j_ happening away from the center of the body
_k_ breaking or blocking of a blood vessel in the brain, often resulting in the loss of some bodily functions

🎧 Outlining practice

An outline gives you a visual picture of the organization of a lecture or reading. In a formal outline, main points are usually designated as I, II, III, etc. Under each main point there are usually supporting points designated as A, B, C, etc. Creating an outline from your notes is a good way to review the material and to show that you understand the relationships between main and supporting points.

1➤ Look at the following incomplete outline of Part One of the lecture. It shows the main points and supporting points you will hear. Read over the outline and try to guess what kind of information you will need in order to complete it.

RISK FACTORS IN CARDIOVASCULAR DISEASE, Part One

I. CVD = heart attacks, strokes, peripheral vascular disease

   A. ♥ attack = _____

   B. _____ = _____

   C. PVD = _____

II. Unalterable risk factors

   A. Gender: Before age 50, ♀ _____

   B. Age: older = _____

   C. _____

   D. _____

2➤ Now listen to Part One of the lecture. Take notes on your own paper. Remember to use symbols and abbreviations as much as possible. 🖭

3➤ Use your notes to complete the outline. You do not need to include everything that you heard; just fill in the blanks.

4➤ Compare outlines with a partner. Did you record the same information?

LECTURE, Part Two: Alterable risk factors in CVD

Guessing vocabulary from context

1➤ The following items contain some important vocabulary from Part Two of the lecture. With a partner, take turns explaining what you think each **boldfaced** term means, based on its context. Even if you can't define a term completely, say as much as you can about it.

_____ *1* There are good medications that have very few **side effects**.

_____ *2* often occurs in people who are **obese**, very overweight

_____ *3* It's very important to get rid of that **excess** weight.

_____ *4* Obese people have trouble **metabolizing** fats.

_____ *5* People who smoke cigarettes have a higher **incidence** of these diseases.

_____ *6* **perfectionist**, competitive person who works very hard and plays very hard

_____ *7* anger and **hostility**

_____ *8* people who react with anger, people who are **hostile**

_____ *9* **Sedentary** lifestyle has just been added as one of the alterable risk factors for cardiovascular disease.

2► Match the vocabulary terms in Step 1 with their definitions by writing the letters in the blanks. Note that some of these terms can have different meanings in other contexts.

a using as body fuel
b very fat
c very unfriendly and ready to fight
d very unfriendly behavior
e extra; more than needed

f very concerned with doing excellent work
g not getting any physical exercise; sitting a lot
h frequency; how often something happens
i unwanted results of taking a medication

🎧 *Outlining practice*

1► Look at the following incomplete outline of Part Two of the lecture. Read over the outline and try to guess what kind of information you will need to complete it.

RISK FACTORS IN CARDIOVASCULAR DISEASE, Part Two

III. _____

    A. HBP – Controlled w/ _____

    B. _____ (≥ 20% _____) may ➔ _____ and _____

    C. _____ ↗ _____

    D. _____

        Type A pers. (= _____)

        Hostility ➔ ↗ _____

    E. Sedentary lifestyle (= _____) ➔ _____

2► Now listen to Part Two of the lecture. Take notes on your own paper. Remember to use symbols and abbreviations as much as possible. 📼

3► Use your notes to complete the outline. Compare outlines with a partner.

AFTER THE LECTURE

Sharing your personal and cultural perspective

Discuss the following questions with a small group of classmates.

1 Is there a high incidence of cardiovascular disease in your country? If yes, which risk factors do you think are responsible? If not, why not, in your opinion?

2 Do you know anyone who fits the Type A description? Which type are you?

3 Do you personally know anyone who has cardiovascular problems? If so, what are that person's risk factors?

4 What about you? Are there any changes that you could make in your lifestyle that would decrease your own risk of cardiovascular disease?

Development Through Life

In this unit you will hear people discuss two stages of human development. Chapter 3 deals with *adolescence*, a difficult and exciting time of life. You will hear an interview with an adolescent girl and her father, and a lecture on the kinds of problems that adolescents sometimes have. Chapter 4 addresses *adulthood*. You will hear people of all ages talk about the challenges and joys of being adults, and you will hear a lecture on *young adulthood*, a period of great personal growth and change.

CHAPTER 3

Adolescence

---

1 GETTING STARTED

In this section you are going to discuss differences in how adolescents grow, and you will record growth rates for a typical American boy and girl.

Reading and thinking about the topic

1➤ Read the following passage.

> Adolescence is a time of great change. The dramatic physical development that comes with adolescence is easy to observe, but the emotional changes and growth are even more important. The adolescent is constantly pushing for more independence, challenging parental control, and experimenting with different attitudes and opinions. This process helps the teenager create his or her own adult identity.
>
> At the same time, adolescents continue to need the support and guidance of their parents. While they often challenge and even disobey parental rules, adolescents still need to know that the rules exist. The parents of an adolescent need to have great patience during this stage in their child's life.

2➤ Answer the following questions according to the information in the passage.

  1 What two kinds of changes occur in adolescence?

  2 What are three examples of adolescent behavior?

  3 Should parents give their teenagers complete freedom? Explain.

3➤ Discuss your own experiences and opinions with a partner.

  1 How much freedom are teenagers given in your culture?

  2 When you were a teenager living at home, were your parents' rules too strict, not strict enough, or just right? Think of examples to support your answers.

Examining visual material

Look at the accompanying pictures. With a partner, discuss what you notice about the relationship between age, height, and gender.

James and Sarah, 10

James and Sarah, 22

🎧 Recording numbers

> **M**any listening tasks involve understanding numbers and writing them down quickly.

1➤ Study the empty graph, where you will record growth rates for James and Sarah. Then listen to the tape and follow the speaker's directions. 📼

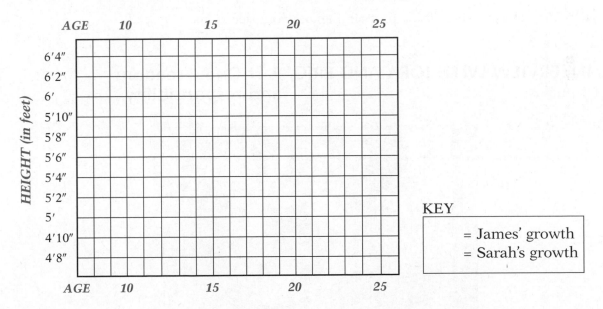

2➤ Work with a partner. One of you will describe James's growth rate, and then the other will describe Sarah's. As you listen to your partner, check that you have the same information on your graph.

3➤ Try to remember your own adolescent height changes and describe them to your partner. Were you ever much taller or much shorter than your peers?

2   AMERICAN VOICES: Jora and Eric

In this section you will hear a three-part interview with Jora, a young teenager, and her father, Eric. They will discuss what Eric lets Jora do and what he doesn't let her do.

BEFORE THE INTERVIEW

Sharing your cultural perspective

1➤ If you were bringing up a daughter in your culture, how much freedom would you give her? Complete the following questionnaire.

HOW STRICT WOULD YOU BE?			
Would you let her . . .	No	Yes	If yes, at what age?
1 wear makeup to school?	____	____	_____
2 choose her own clothes?	____	____	_____
3 go out with boys?	____	____	_____
4 watch R-rated movies?	____	____	_____
5 dye her hair?	____	____	_____

2➤ Compare answers with a partner. Explain your decisions.

INTERVIEW WITH JORA AND ERIC, Part One: Freedom
and responsibility

Eric and Jora

Here are some words and phrases from Part One of the interview, printed in **boldface** and given in the context in which you will hear them. They are followed by definitions.

***see** it **from a different perspective**:* have a different opinion
*as much freedom as she can **handle**:* accept; use responsibly
***has acted responsibly**:* has been careful; has behaved wisely

🎧 Listening for specific information: Script writing

1➤ Before you listen to Part One of the interview, read these incomplete scripts of two conversations between Jora and her father. Try to imagine words that would complete the conversations.

Jora: Dad, can you drive _____ tonight?

Eric: I can drive you there, but I can't pick you up. How will you _____ ?

Jora: We can _____ .

Eric: _____ .

. . .

Jora: Dad, why are you so strict!? You never give me any _____ !

Eric: Jora, I'll give you more _____ when you show me that you can _____ .

Jora: How can I do that?

Eric: Well, for example, if I ask you to _____ , you need to _____ . Or if

you are in any kind of trouble, _____ .

2➤ Now listen to Part One of the interview. You will hear Jora and Eric talk about having these conversations. Listen specifically for information that will help you complete the scripts. After you listen, complete them. 📼

Jora (top left) with her friends

3➤ Compare scripts with a partner. Your scripts do not have to be exactly the same. Ask your teacher for help if you need to.

INTERVIEW WITH JORA AND ERIC, Part Two: Clothes and makeup

> Here are some words and phrases from Part Two of the interview.
>
> *Does he **put his foot down?**:* absolutely refuse to permit something in a very strict way (informal)
>
> ***bell bottoms****:* a style of pants popular in the 1960s
>
> ***You're not gonna*** _____ *(verb),* ***period****:* You may *not*. That is my final decision. (informal)
>
> *a **square***: an old-fashioned person, or one who wears old-fashioned clothes (slang)
>
> *a **hippie***: one who believes in freedom from social rules, sometimes a drug user
>
> *a **drug culture***: a group of people (here, teenagers) who use drugs
>
> ***gang clothes****:* a style of clothing first worn by teenage gang members, usually very large and loose (to hide weapons)
>
> *My dad **has loosened up***: become less strict, more permissive
>
> *Just because he says no,* ***I'm not gonna not*** _____ *(verb):* I won't agree not to (informal)
>
> ***behind our backs****:* secretly, without our permission

🎧 Listening for main ideas

> **I**n an informal interview or conversation, people express their main points gradually, in bits, not as an organized list. When listening to conversation, you must put together everything people have said in order to figure out what they really want to express.

1➤ Read the following statements before you listen to Part Two of the interview.

1 Jora doesn't agree / generally agrees that she has enough control over what she wears.

2 Eric's mother and father were stricter / less strict than Eric is as a parent.

3 Eric's parents were worried about drugs, and so is Eric. / but Eric isn't.

4 Jora never / sometimes disobeys her parents' rules.

5 Eric's parents didn't discuss their rules with their child, and neither does Eric. / but Eric does.

2➤ Now listen to Part Two of the interview with Jora and Eric. Circle the correct words in Step 1 to make the statements true. 🎞️

3➤ Compare answers with a partner and then as a class.

INTERVIEW WITH JORA AND ERIC, Part Three: Different parents, different rules

> Here are some words and phrases from Part Three of the interview.
>
> ***stuff****:* things or issues (slang)
>
> ***PG-13*** *movies:* acceptable for thirteen-year-olds, if a parent approves (PG = parental guidance)
>
> ***R-rated*** *movies:* not acceptable for anyone under the age of eighteen (R = restricted)
>
> ***looser****:* less strict
>
> ***chores****:* household jobs that children are required to do (e.g., washing dishes, making beds, cleaning)
>
> *an* ***allowance****:* sum of money given to children by their parents, usually every week

🎧 *Summarizing what you have heard*

1➤ Read the incomplete summary before you listen to Part Three of the interview. Try to predict what might fit in the blanks.

> Jora agrees that her father is _____, but _____. When he won't let her do something, at first she is _____, but later she usually _____ . Jora's mother (who is divorced from Eric) is _____ strict than Eric about some things, such as _____ . Jora says that Eric won't let _____ _____ movies, but her mother _____ _____ . However, her mother is stricter about _____, _____, and _____ . For example, she wants Jora to pay for _____ . In conclusion, Jora says that Eric lets her do "_____."

2➤ Now listen to Part Three of the interview with Jora and Eric. Complete the summary. 🎞️

3➤ Compare summaries with a partner. You do not need to have the same words. Ask your teacher for help if you need to.

AFTER THE INTERVIEW

Drawing inferences

1➤ Read the following statements and decide whether you agree (*A*) or disagree (*D*) with each one. Be ready to give evidence from the interview to support your opinion.

_____ *1* Eric takes his role as father seriously.

_____ *2* Jora does not respect her father.

_____ *3* Jora thinks both her parents are too strict.

_____ *4* Eric enjoys being a father.

_____ *5* Eric didn't like the way his parents disciplined him.

2➤ Compare opinions with one or two classmates. Explain your reasoning.

Looking at the cultural context

It is helpful when examining a single case – such as Eric and Jora's – to look at the broader cultural picture as well.

1➤ Read the paragraph and discuss the following questions with one or two classmates.

> Eric and Jora's mother are divorced, and Jora divides her time between her parents. Her situation is not unusual in the United States. In 1995, about 26 percent of U.S. households with children under eighteen had only a mother at home. Four percent had only a father.

1 How do you think having only one parent at home has affected Jora?

2 Have any of the effects been positive, in your opinion?

2➤ The following information from *The New York Times Magazine* outlines some of the difficulties faced by American adolescents and their parents. Read the statistics and discuss them in your small group.

> *Among twelve- to thirteen-year-olds in the United States:*
>
> • 70% know someone their age who smokes.
> • 44%   "   "   "   "   " drinks.
> • 33%   "   "   "   "   " uses drugs.
> • 29%   "   "   "   "   " has a gun.
> • 27%   "   "   "   "   " has been to jail.
> • 20%   "   "   "   "   " has a child or is pregnant.

1 What do the statistics tell you about adolescents in the United States?

2 Which, if any, of the issues mentioned are problems in your country?

3 IN YOUR OWN VOICE

In this section you will do some research on the topic of adolescence.

Sharing your personal perspective

> **T**alking about your personal perspective on a topic is a good way to review the topic and to deepen your understanding of it.

Interview a classmate about his or her early teenage years. If possible, interview someone from a different culture. You may want to use the example questions in the box. Add other questions of your own.

Did you enjoy your early teenage years?

What was good or not so good about them?

Did you experience a lot of peer pressure?

How strict were your parents?

Giving an oral presentation

> **W**hen you give an informal speech, remember the following:
>
> • Do not read your speech. Use notes and make eye contact with your audience.
> • Use language that you are sure your classmates will understand, and explain any terms that you think may be unfamiliar to them.
> • Use pictures, charts, and other aids to clarify important points.
> • Be ready to answer questions about what you have said.

1➤ Interview a parent of a teenage child about raising a teenager. Prepare your questions first. To get ideas for questions, think about the interview with Jora and Eric. You may want to use the example questions in the box. Add questions of your own.

How much freedom do you like to give your daughter/son?

Are you stricter or less strict than your parents were?

Does your daughter/son ever do things behind your back?

2➤ Take notes during the interview. Ask your interviewee for specific examples.

3➤ Give a brief oral presentation about what you learned.

4 ACADEMIC LISTENING AND NOTE TAKING: Common problems of adolescents in mental health treatment

In this section you will hear and take notes on a two-part lecture given by Marjorie Katz, a licensed psychotherapist who works with adolescents. The title of the lecture is *Common Problems of Adolescents in Mental Health Treatment*. Ms. Katz will discuss two problems that she sees frequently in her work with teenagers.

BEFORE THE LECTURE

Predicting the content

1➤ Try to predict what kind of behavior teachers or parents might notice that would make them decide to send a teenager to a therapist for guidance or counseling. Write your ideas in the boxes.

A teacher might notice:	A parent might notice:
not doing homework	

2➤ Compare ideas as a class. If you hear new ideas, add them to your lists.

Looking for causes

> In almost any academic discipline – from biology to history to adolescent psychology – in order to understand the facts, it is essential to go beyond what we hear or observe and ask *why*.

1➤ The two problems that Ms. Katz will discuss in her lecture are (a) alcohol and drug abuse and (b) poor school performance. With a partner, discuss what might cause a teenager to get involved with alcohol or drugs, or to stop caring about school.

2➤ Compare ideas as a class.

🎧 *Note taking: Using space to show organizational structure*

As you listen to a lecture and take notes, your goal is to understand the lecture and to produce a written record of what was said. However, your notes should not be simply a list of the ideas presented in the lecture. They should also reflect the structure of the lecture: how the points relate to each other, which points are general, and which are specific.

As a note taker, then, you have to listen for two things at the same time: You must listen for the *content* of the lecture, and you must also pay attention to its *structure*, and record it as accurately as possible.

One way to record the structure of a lecture is with a formal outline, as in Chapter 2. But there is an easier way: When you take notes, you can show how ideas are related by your use of blank space on the page. List the general points along the left-hand margin of the page. Leave some blank space below each point so that it will be easy to locate these main ideas when you review your notes after the lecture. (You can also use the space to add details or explanation later on.) Then indent as you list the more specific ideas and examples. Continue to indent each time the lecture moves from more general to more specific, as shown in the following model:

The first general point

    A specific point related to the first general point
    A second specific point related to the first general point
       A detail about the second specific point (an example, a statistic, etc.)
  The second general point
    (etc.)

By using the space on the page in this way, you will be able to see the organizational structure of the lecture at a glance when you go over your notes. Your notes will be a useful tool for reviewing the information presented in the lecture.

1➤ The following notes were taken by a student listening to an excerpt from Part Two of Ms. Katz's lecture. One point is very general. Two other points are more specific and should be indented. The remaining points are even more specific and should be indented further. Read the notes and try to decide which point is the most general, which two points are a little more specific, and so on. Be sure that you understand the abbreviations used.

2nd prob. – school (= failing, acting out, not going to class)

reasons

younger bros. & sisters – parents busy

teens have diffic. – need to rely on parents

treatment

get parents involved

par. need to give <u>structure</u>

clear rules for behav.

discipl. if teen breaks rules

2► Now listen to the excerpt from the lecture and mark which points in the notes in Step 1 should be indented. [cassette icon]

3► Recopy the notes on your own paper, indenting the points as you marked them. Leave space between lines so you can add to your notes later.

4► Compare notes with a partner. You will need these notes later, so save them.

LECTURE, Part One: Adolescent alcohol and drug abuse

Guessing vocabulary from context

1► The following terms from Part One of the lecture are shown in **boldface** in the contexts in which you will hear them. Work with a partner. Using context, take turns guessing the meanings.

_____ *1* problems at school, including **acting out**, poor academic performance, and truancy

_____ *2* acting out, poor academic performance, and **truancy**

_____ *3* not just **recreational** use of drugs

_____ *4* **severe**, long-term addictions

_____ *5* children who have been physically **abused** and who have negative feelings

_____ *6* The only way to **blunt** their negative feelings is with drugs.

_____ *7* a hospital stay for them to **detoxify**

_____ *8* develop the **coping skills** to resist the urge to go back to drugs

_____ *9* coping skills to **resist** the urge to go back to drugs

_____ *10* people in treatment or **recovery** programs

_____ *11* adolescents who have recovered from **substance abuse**

_____ *12* they might feel very angry and want **revenge** if it was physical abuse

_____ *13* go through months of therapy and remain **sober**

_____ *14* a great deal of the therapist's help consists of **nonjudgmental** acceptance

2► Match the terms in Step 1 with their definitions by writing the letters in the blanks. Note that the definitions reflect the way the terms are used in the lecture; some of these terms can have different meanings in other contexts.

a treated badly, sometimes beaten
b clean drugs out of the body
c say no to
d addiction to a drug

e very bad; very strong
f just for fun and enjoyment
g behaving badly; being disruptive
h without criticism or negative reaction
i not drunk; free of alcohol or drugs
j cause to feel less; dull, usually a pain
k the process of getting over an addiction
l act of hurting someone who has hurt you
m not going to school; skipping classes
n ability to handle a difficult situation

Note-taking practice

1► The following is an incomplete set of student notes for Part One of the lecture. The student has indented to give visual clues to the organization and content. Read the notes and notice how the lecture is organized. Try to predict what you might write in the blanks.

Common probs. of adols. in mental health treatment (Pt. 1)

Discuss 2 problems of adols.

= _____ & _____

Talk abt. reasons, then possible _____

1st prob. = _____

   Reasons = usually _____

    Adol. takes drugs to _____

  Treatment = _____ & difficult

   Hospital 1st: _____

   Group work: _____

   After 30–60 days, adol. ready to _____ . May feel _____

    Important! Therapist must _____

    Takes a long time: _____

    If teen can _____ , good chance _____

2► Now listen to Part One of the lecture. Take notes on your own paper. Remember to use symbols and abbreviations, and indent as the lecturer moves from the general to the specific.

3► Use your notes to complete the student notes in the box.

4► Compare notes on this page with a partner. They do not have to be exactly the same.

LECTURE, Part Two: Common problems related to school

Guessing vocabulary from context

1➤ The following items contain some important vocabulary from Part Two of the lecture. Work with a partner. Using context, take turns trying to guess the meanings.

_____ 1 sometimes there are younger **siblings** at home

_____ 2 give teenagers a chance to **prove themselves** on their own

_____ 3 give teenagers a chance to prove themselves **on their own**

_____ 4 letting the parents know that more attention and more **structure** are needed

_____ 5 parents **follow through** with discipline if the child fails to meet expectations

_____ 6 parents follow through with **discipline** if the child fails to meet expectations

_____ 7 Adolescents are **struggling with** who they are, what they can do.

_____ 8 if family life is not providing this basic **nurturing**

2➤ Match the vocabulary terms in Step 1 with their definitions by writing the letters in the blanks.

_a_ trying to understand or figure out
_b_ brothers and sisters
_c_ loving support; help and understanding
_d_ clear rules for how to act

_e_ do what one promised to do
_f_ show what they can do without help
_g_ punishment
_h_ independently; without help

🎧 Note-taking practice

1➤ In the task, _Note taking: Using space to show organizational structure_, on page 41, you heard excerpts from Part Two of the lecture and worked on some notes on the excerpts that you heard. Read those notes again before you listen to the complete version of Part Two.

2➤ Now listen to the complete version of Part Two. Add to your notes as you listen, and listen carefully for the conclusion. Remember to indent as the lecturer moves from the general to the specific. Use abbreviations and symbols to save time. 📼

3➤ Compare notes with a partner. They do not have to be exactly the same.

AFTER THE LECTURE

Sharing your cultural perspective

Discuss the following questions in a small group.

1 Is it common for teenagers in your country to go to psychotherapy?

2 In your country, how do parents respond to teenagers who start having problems in school? How do schools respond?

3 What do *you* think is the best way to deal with the problems presented in this lecture?

Considering related information

> The more information you can hear or read about a topic, the deeper will be your understanding of it.

1➤ Read the following information from *Newsweek* magazine.

A poll was taken of 758 children between the ages of 10 and 17 and their parents. The children were asked who had a "very important" influence on them, and the parents were asked who had influenced them when they were their children's age. Here are the results.

Children		*Parents*
86%	Their parents	81%
56%	Grandparents	47%
55%	Place of worship	55%
50%	Teachers	48%
41%	Children their own age	37%
23%	Community organizations	17%
22%	TV, movies, and music	20%

2➤ Answer the following questions in a small group.

1 How do the answers of children and their parents compare?

2 What conclusions can you draw from this poll?

3 How would you respond to the poll? Which were the greatest influences on you?

CHAPTER 4

Adulthood

1   GETTING STARTED

In this section you are going to discuss different stages of adulthood, and you will hear American adults of different ages answer the question, "In your opinion, what is the best age to be?"

Reading and thinking about the topic

1➤ Read the following passage.

> The period that we call *adulthood* covers most of our lives. It begins with *young* adulthood, a time of many difficult but exciting decisions: What career should I pursue? Where should I live? Should I get married? What about children?
>
> The years of *middle* adulthood bring other changes and challenges: Our bodies are beginning to show signs of age, and our children and our parents are entering new stages of their lives.
>
> Finally, *late* adulthood, too, is a time of difficult transition. Our bodies have slowed down. Friends, siblings, and spouses are getting sick and dying. Children have grown up and become independent. However, late adulthood brings its own rewards as well: Retirement provides time to enjoy grandchildren, hobbies, and travel.

2➤ Answer the following questions according to the information in the passage.

1 What are the three stages of adulthood mentioned in the passage?

2 How does the reading characterize each of the three stages?

3➤ Discuss your own experiences and opinions with a partner.

1 The passage describes young adulthood in the United States as a time of decision making. What differences (if any) are there in the kinds of decisions that young adults have to make in your culture?

2 Do you consider yourself an adult? Explain.

Predicting the content

1➤ How would you expect people of different ages to answer the question "What is the best age to be?" Complete the following chart with your guesses.

I think that . . .	would say that . . .	is the best age to be.
a man in his late 20s	_____	
a woman in her mid-20s	_____	
an elderly man	_____	
an elderly woman	_____	
a middle-aged man (40s–50s)	_____	
a middle-aged woman (40s–50s)	_____	

2➤ Compare guesses with a partner. Explain your choices.

🎧 Recording numbers

1➤ Listen to the tape and follow the speaker's directions. 📼

Name	Age Now	The Best Age
Bruce	_____	_____
Julie	_____	_____
Ann	_____	_____
David	_____	_____
Otis	_____	_____
Laurie	_____	_____
Gene	_____	_____
Loleta	_____	_____

2➤ Compare numbers with a partner. Do you agree?

3➤ Look back at your predictions. How accurate were you?

4➤ Conduct a survey of your class. Find out what everyone thinks is the best age to be.

2 AMERICAN VOICES: The best age to be

In this section you will hear the reasons given by some of the people you listened to in Section 1 for "the best age" that they named.

BEFORE THE SURVEY

Predicting the content

Discuss the following questions with one or two classmates.

 1 Why do you think Bruce says that his current years are his best years?
 2 Why might Julie want to be a little child again?
 3 Why do you think Otis says that his forties were his best years?
 4 What might be Laurie's reasons for saying "My forties were *wonderful*"?

SURVEY, Part One: Bruce, Julie, and Ann

Here are some words and expressions used in Part One of the survey, printed in **boldface** and given in the context in which you will hear them. They are followed by definitions.

*You **kinda** know a direction:* kind of; more or less; somewhat but not completely (informal)

*You know how to **settle down**:* get a job, buy a house, get married, etc.

*You **pretty much** know what you like:* almost completely; more than *kind of* (informal)

*You're kind of **settled** into life:* stable; secure; in a more or less permanent situation

actually, *now that my sons are married:* a word used to introduce an opposite or unexpected fact or idea

when I come to think about *(or* ***of****) it:* an expression used when we change our minds or get a new idea as we are speaking

⌂ Answering true/false questions

> When answering true/false questions, remember that a correct negative statement is true. Also, if any part of a statement is false, the entire statement is false.

1➤ Read the following statements about Part One of the survey. Make sure that you understand the negative statements.

_____ *1* Bruce feels ready to settle down now.

_____ *2* Bruce says that in the early twenties you think too much about the future.

_____ 3 Bruce thinks that the adolescent years were the hardest.

_____ 4 Julie says that her childhood was not as relaxed as her mid-twenties.

_____ 5 Julie is trying to get used to all her new responsibilities.

_____ 6 Julie's parents don't take care of her anymore.

_____ 7 Ann felt settled in her thirties.

_____ 8 Ann changes her mind about the best age as she is speaking.

_____ 9 Ann does more things for her children now that she is older.

Bruce

Julie

Ann

2► Now listen to Part One of the survey. Write *T* (true) or *F* (false) next to the statements in Step 1. 🖭

3► Compare answers with a partner. Correct the false statements together. Now look back at your guesses about Bruce and Julie in *Predicting the content*. Were they correct?

SURVEY, Part Two: Otis, Laurie, and Gene

> Here are some words and expressions used in Part Two of the survey.
>
> *much more **receptive** to new ideas:* open; willing to accept
>
> *Most of them **worked**:* were successful
>
> *'**cuz** I hadn't done that before:* because (informal)
>
> *I got my **master's degree**:* graduate degree usually requiring two to three years of study
>
> *free of my **commitments**:* responsibilities; things that a person has promised to do
>
> ***The older you get, the more you think about your youth**:* As you get older and older, you think more and more about when you were young.
>
> *What **an idiot** I was:* a fool, a crazy person (slang)
>
> *when you're younger, **for instance**:* for example
>
> *Your **joints** hurt:* knees, shoulders, elbows, ankles, for example

☊ Summarizing what you have heard

1➤ Read the following incomplete summaries before you listen to Part Two of the survey.

Otis is a retired university professor. He says that his best teaching years were between _____ and _____ because he was more open to new ideas, he _____ , and _____ . At the age of _____ , he created _____ . However, Otis feels that in another sense, his last _____ years have been the best because _____ .

Otis

Laurie and Gene

Laurie and Gene are married. They are both painters. Laurie remembers her _____ as a great time because she got her master's degree, she _____ , and _____ _____ .

Gene says that the older he gets, the _____ . Especially when he wakes up in the morning, he notices that _____ . He and Laurie talk about how long _____ _____ . When he was a young man, in the Army, he used to _____ . But now _____ .

2➤ Now listen to Part Two of the survey. Complete the summaries. 🔳

3➤ Compare summaries with a partner. Your answers do not have to be exactly the same. Were your guesses about Otis and Laurie in *Predicting the content* correct?

AFTER THE SURVEY

Creating a chart

> **M**aking a chart of the main points of a lecture or conversation is a good way to review the material, and it will also help you to remember the information.

As a class, recall what Bruce, Julie, Ann, and the others said about the various stages of life. Summarize the good points, changes, and challenges that they mentioned. Enter them next to the appropriate ages in the accompanying box.

Childhood	no worries,
Teens	
20s	
30s	feel settled,
40s	
50s	
Late adulthood	

3 IN YOUR OWN VOICE

In this section you will give your own cultural perspective on the different stages of adulthood, and you will conduct a survey outside of class.

Sharing your cultural perspective

Work in a small group – with classmates from different cultures, if possible. Examine the information in the task *Creating a chart* in Section 2, American Voices. Think about the attitudes toward the various stages of life expressed by the Americans surveyed. How are these attitudes different from those of people in your culture? How are they similar? Make generalizations.

> *Americans tend to see middle age as a time of freedom from the responsibilities of parenthood. In my culture, . . .*

Conducting a survey

1➤ Work with a partner. Together, survey twenty people from outside your class. (See the task *Conducting a survey* in Chapter 2, Section 3, for guidelines on surveys.) Ask the same questions that you heard in the taped survey ("What do you think is the best age, and why?"). Do *not* ask people their ages unless you know them well. In some cultures, including that of the United States, it is impolite to ask the age of a person whom you do not know well. Record people's approximate age (20s, 30s, etc.) and their gender.

2➤ Analyze your results and share them with your class.

Childhood

Young adulthood

Late adulthood

4   ACADEMIC LISTENING AND NOTE TAKING: Developmental tasks of early adulthood

In this section you will hear and take notes on a lecture given by Anthony Brown, a psychotherapist and professor of psychology. The title of the lecture is *Developmental Tasks of Early Adulthood*. Professor Brown will discuss the important decisions and life changes that young adults have to make.

BEFORE THE LECTURE

Building background knowledge on the topic

1➤ In many academic courses, the professor will assign textbook reading on the same topic as the lecture. Professor Brown wants his students to read Chapter 6, "Young Adulthood," in their textbooks before the lecture. Look at the description of Chapter 6 in the table of contents of the course textbook.

2➤ Chapter 6 is about the major developmental tasks of young adulthood. The general meaning of the first task in the table of contents is clear, but the second one uses special terminology. Let's read an excerpt from Chapter 6 to find an explanation of the terms.

> German psychologist Erik Erikson (1902–1994) theorized that the human personality develops in eight stages throughout life. These stages are not so much periods of time as they are a series of conflicts, or crises, that need to be resolved. [. . .] Stage Six: the crisis of *intimacy versus isolation*. If the adult has achieved a sense of identity, then she can form close relationships and share with others. Failure at this stage consists of being unable to relate intimately to others. The person may develop a sense of isolation, feeling there is no one but herself she can depend on in the world.

3➤ Answer the following questions with a partner.

1 How do you think a person accomplishes the first task (separation from parents)?

2 Who was Erik Erikson?

3 What does *versus* mean, and why is it used in the expression *intimacy versus isolation*?

4 How does the excerpt describe intimacy? isolation?

🎧 Note taking: Paying attention to signal words

As you are reading a text, you can *see* how it is organized. You can read section headings to guess the general topic, look at the paragraph divisions to find main points, and scan for signal words like *the most important*, and *first, second,* and *finally*, to get clues to the organization of the text. Most important, you can reread the text as many times as you need to.

However, in a lecture, you cannot hear paragraph divisions, you cannot scan for signal words, and you have no chance to listen to the lecture again. Fortunately, lecturers do use signal words like *first* and *finally*, and these structural cues allow you to hear how the lecture is organized as you are listening. When you can hear the organization, you can often predict what will come next, and as a result your notes will be more complete and accurate.

You probably know the more common signal words, words like *because, however, as a result, so,* and *first*. But there are many other words and expressions that can act as road signs, helping you predict what kind of information will follow. Some of them signal that a definition is going to follow. Others indicate that the speaker is going to repeat a point. Some of the signal words that you will hear in a lecture are commonly found in both written and spoken English. But others (such as the expression, *as I said*) are generally limited to spoken English.

1➤ Here are some important signal words, printed in **boldface** and presented in the context in which you will hear them in the lecture. What kind of information do you expect will follow each one? Read the descriptions below, and match them to the signal words by writing the letters in the blanks to the left of the numbers. You will use one letter twice.

_____ *1* and **by** developmental tasks **I mean** _____

_____ *2* supporting himself completely – **that includes** _____

_____ *3* in a hierarchical way, **that is** _____

_____ *4* **the result is** that _____

_____ *5* **So, as I said,** _____

_____ *6* **But even though** it's natural, _____

_____ *7* **So we've talked about** _____

a a contrasting fact or idea
b a definition
c details
d repetition of a point
e the effect of the facts or processes just described
f a summary of main points

2➤ Compare answers as a class.

3▶ Now listen to the excerpts that you have just read, and find out what information follows each of the signal words. Take notes in the blanks provided in Step 1. Remember to use symbols and abbreviations. Do not write unnecessary words. ▭

4▶ Work with your partner. Use your notes to reconstruct orally what you heard.

LECTURE, Part One: Separation from parents

Guessing vocabulary from context

1▶ The following items contain some important vocabulary from Part One of the lecture. Each of the terms is in **boldface** in the context in which you will hear it. Work with a partner. Using context, take turns trying to guess the meanings.

Psychologist Erik Erikson

_____ 1 By **developmental tasks** I mean the life changes that a person must accomplish.

_____ 2 Ideally, what's considered **optimal** is for the young adult to be capable of supporting himself or herself.

_____ 3 the old relationship, in which the child related to his parents in a **hierarchical way**, that is, solely as parents

_____ 4 The child related to his parents in a hierarchical way, that is, **solely** as parents.

_____ 5 a new kind of relationship based on **mutual** adulthood

_____ 6 the sort of **culmination** of a long process of separation

_____ 7 Even though it's natural, this is still a **crisis point**, when a child leaves.

2▶ Match the terms in Step 1 with their definitions by writing the letters in the blanks. Note that the definitions reflect the way the terms are used in the lecture; some of these terms can have different meanings in other contexts.

a structured so that people have higher and lower positions
b things that one must accomplish in order to grow up successfully
c end point; conclusion
d felt or agreed to by both people
e only
f the best; ideal
g difficult period in life when one must make a change

🎧 Note-taking practice

1➤ The following are incomplete notes for Part One of the lecture. Try to predict what information you will need to listen for. Pay attention to indenting, and remember that the points on the far left are the most general.

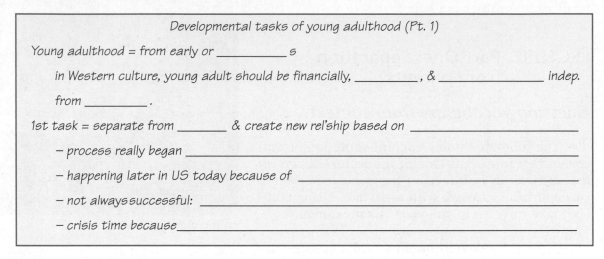

Developmental tasks of young adulthood (Pt. 1)

Young adulthood = from early or _____ s

    in Western culture, young adult should be financially, _____ , & _____ indep.

    from _____ .

1st task = separate from _____ & create new rel'ship based on _____

    – process really began _____

    – happening later in US today because of _____

    – not always successful: _____

    – crisis time because_____

2➤ Now listen to Part One of the lecture. Take notes on your own paper. 📼

3➤ Use your notes to fill in the blanks. Then compare notes with a partner.

LECTURE, Part Two: The crisis of intimacy versus isolation

Guessing vocabulary from context

1➤ The following items contain some important vocabulary from Part Two of the lecture. Work with a partner. Using context, take turns trying to guess the meanings.

_____ *1* The young adult faces the crisis of **intimacy** versus isolation.

_____ *2* the crisis of intimacy versus **isolation**

_____ *3* Healthy people during this period are able to **compromise**, to sacrifice, to negotiate, all of which one must do to make a marriage successful.

_____ *4* able to compromise, to **sacrifice**, to negotiate, all of which one must do to make a marriage successful

_____ *5* to compromise, to sacrifice, to **negotiate**, all of which one must do to make a marriage successful

_____ *6* Staying single has become an acceptable **alternative** to marriage.

_____ *7* With the divorce rate as high as it is, there is a certain **reluctance** about marriage as an institution.

_____ *8* a certain reluctance, a **skepticism** about marriage as an institution

2► Match the terms in Step 1 with these definitions.

a feeling of doubt; lack of trust

b give up something one wants

c hesitation to do something

d physical and emotional closeness

e being alone

f different choice; option

g discuss differences with the hope of coming to an agreement

h come to an agreement, usually with both sides accepting less than what they wanted

🎧 Note-taking practice

1► The following are incomplete student notes for Part Two of the lecture. Read them and try to predict what information you will need to listen for.

Developmental tasks of young adulthood (Pt. 2)

2nd task – traditionally leads to _____

　*called "crisis of _____ "

　If child develops _____ identity in adolescence → able to
　_____ in young _____ .

　　　– person must be able to compromise, _____ , _____ .

　　　– if successful → _____

　　　– if not succ. → _____

　　　– success depends on _____

　Alternative to marriage today: staying single longer

　　have freedom _____

　　skepticism _____

　　　→ wait until _____ → much lower_____

　If young adults succeed at these 2 tasks → _____

2► Now listen to **Part Two** of the lecture. Complete the student notes as you listen. 📼

3► Compare notes with a partner. They do not have to be exactly the same.

"He has a few things to work through, but we're good together."

AFTER THE LECTURE

Applying general concepts to specific data

> **A** good way to check your understanding of an abstract concept such as *separation* or *intimacy versus isolation* is to try to apply it to some specific circumstances or data.

1➤ Which two people surveyed in Section 2, American Voices, are young adults? Do you think they both have successfully separated from their parents? Discuss with a partner.

2➤ Read the following statistical data about changes in the American family, and answer the questions with a partner or in a small group.

> In 1970, 7.3 million American women lived alone; in 1995, 14.6 million did.
>
> In 1970, 3.5 million American men lived alone; in 1995, 10.2 million did.
>
> In 1970, the median age for men to marry was 23.2; in 1994, it was 26.7.
>
> In 1970, the median age for women to marry was 20.8; in 1994, it was 24.5.
>
> In 1970, 6% of women and 9% of men ages 30 to 34 had never been married; in 1994, 20% of women and 30% of men ages 30 to 34 had never been married.
>
> In 1970, the ratio of marriages to divorces was 3 to 1; in 1995, it was 2 to 1.

1 Do you see any data that supports what Professor Brown said about the process of separation from parents in the late twentieth century?

2 Do you think the data can tell us anything about *intimacy versus isolation*?

Sharing your personal and cultural perspective

Discuss the following questions with a classmate or in a small group.

1➤ Read the following quotation from the lecture.

> Ideally, what's considered optimal is for the young adult to be capable of supporting him- or herself completely – that includes financially, psychologically, and socially.

The idea that we must separate from our parents before we can be adults is a Western concept, and it may not apply at all in other cultures. Does it mean anything in your culture? What expectations does your culture have of young adults?

2➤ In your opinion, what is good about Western cultural expectations of young adults? What is not good? Explain and support your reasoning.

In this unit you will hear people discuss topics related to intelligence. Chapter 5 deals with how we measure intelligence. You will hear the author in conversation with a childhood friend and schoolmate. You will also hear a lecture on the history of intelligence testing. Chapter 6, on accounting for variations in intelligence, includes an interview with a public school administrator and a lecture on factors influencing the development of intelligence.

CHAPTER 5

Assessing Intelligence

---

1 GETTING STARTED

In this section you will discuss the meaning of intelligence and answer a series of questions like those used to measure intelligence on standardized tests in the United States.

Reading and thinking about the topic

1➤ Read the following passage.

> What does it mean to be intelligent? Definitions vary. The psychologist David Wechsler defined intelligence as "the capacity of an individual to understand the world about him/her and his/her resourcefulness to cope with its challenges."
>
> How do we measure an individual's intelligence? Most Americans would say that we measure intelligence with an IQ (Intelligence Quotient) test. However, there is disagreement about what exactly an IQ score means and how it should be used. For example, does an IQ test provide any useful information about how successful a person will be in school? What about in life? in work?

2➤ Answer the following questions according to the information in the passage.

 1 What are the two parts of Wechsler's definition of intelligence?
 2 What questions do people have about the value of IQ scores?

3➤ Discuss your own experiences and opinions with a partner.

 1 Think of someone whom you consider intelligent. What qualities does the person have that make you think of him or her as intelligent?
 2 Have you ever taken an intelligence test? If yes, do you remember what kinds of questions it asked?

ᐧᓃ Listening to directions

1► Listen to the tape and follow the speaker's directions. ▭

1 _____ 2 _____

3 _____ 4 _____ 5–6 (*say your answers aloud*)

7 _____
_____
_____

8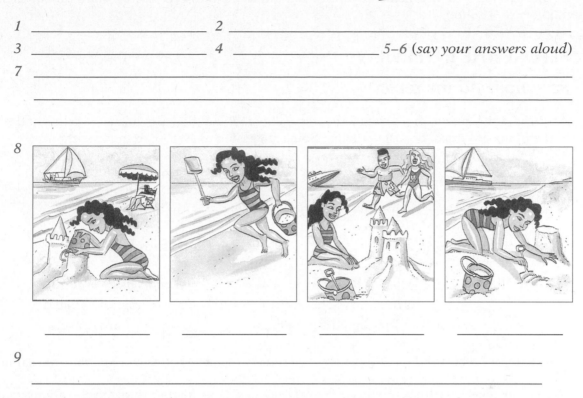

_____ _____ _____ _____

9 _____
_____

2► Compare answers with a partner. Do you agree? Are your definitions similar?

3► The short test you just took had several different types of questions. Discuss with a partner what skill you think each group of questions was testing. Write down your guesses.

1 _____
2 _____
3–4 _____
5–6 _____
7 _____
8 _____
9 _____

4► Make up a few test questions similar to questions 5 and 6 for your partner. Prepare sets of eight numbers for your partner to say forward and sets of six numbers for your partner to say backward. Repeat your numbers to each other. Also, try the same exercise with words instead of numbers.

2   AMERICAN VOICES: Ruth

In this section you will hear the author talking to a childhood friend, Ruth, about their memories of school.

BEFORE THE INTERVIEW

Personalizing the topic

1➤ What are your memories of elementary school? Read the following statements and fill in the blanks to make true statements. Some suggested answers are in parentheses ( ).

1 _____ was/were easy for me. (math/languages/writing/nothing/ everything)

2 I _____ helped my sibling(s) (or friends) with homework. (never/sometimes, etc.)

3 My sibling(s) (or friends) _____ helped me with homework. (never/sometimes, etc.)

4 I studied _____ for my classes. (a lot/very little/an average amount)

5 I _____ elementary school. (loved/usually enjoyed/tolerated/hated)

6 In elementary school I thought of myself as _____ . (smart/average/ stupid)

7 As I got older, I did _____ in most subjects. (better/worse/about the same)

2➤ Share answers with a small group of classmates. Give further information about your answers if you like.

INTERVIEW WITH RUTH, Part One: Being a "smart kid"

> Here are some words and expressions from Part One of the interview, printed in **boldface** and given in the context in which you will hear them. They are followed by definitions.
>
> *the **so-called** "smart kids":* believed to be (intelligent) by most people. The speaker doesn't necessarily agree.
>
> ***the first reading group**:* the group of students who could read the best
>
> *I remember **vividly**:* very clearly; very well
>
> *My brother **struggled with** spelling:* had a hard time with; could not do easily
>
> ***irregular** spellings:* not following the rules (e.g., *people* has an irregular spelling)
>
> *He could not **get** it:* understand
>
> *I **threw my hands up**:* gave up; stopped trying

🎧 Listening for specific information

1➤ Read the following questions before you listen to Part One of the interview.

1 Which reading group was Ruth in when she was in elementary school?

2 What kinds of questions did other children ask her?

3 Is Ruth's brother older or younger than she is?

4 What was difficult for him?

5 How did Ruth remember irregular spellings?

6 Was Ruth able to help her brother?

2➤ Listen to Part One of the interview. Write short answers to the questions in Step 1. 📼

3➤ Compare answers with a partner.

THE FAR SIDE   By GARY LARSON

Primitive spelling bees

INTERVIEW WITH RUTH, Part Two: A subject she "didn't get"

Here are some words and expressions from Part Two of the interview.

basically *without trying:* in general; for the most part (informal)

It was **positive** *for me:* enjoyable; good

all of a sudden: suddenly; unexpectedly

I **encountered** *something:* met; faced; had to deal with

You either got it or you didn't: If you didn't understand it at first, you would never understand it.

I **floundered through**: continued to study but did very badly and did not understand

I was always **fascinated by** *mathematics:* very interested in; attracted to

I had a lot of **rapport** *with them:* a friendly feeling and good understanding between people

I **labeled** *myself as not good at [algebra]:* made a (usually negative) judgment about

🎧 Listening for specific information

1➤ Read the following four questions before you listen to Part Two of the interview.

1 When did Ruth start to have trouble in school, and with what subject?

2 What did she do when this happened?

3 What happened later in college?

4 In what way did Ruth "label" herself, and when did she do this?

2➤ Now listen to Part Two of the interview. Write short answers to the questions in Step 1. 📼

3➤ Compare answers with a partner.

Ruth, 1971

INTERVIEW WITH RUTH, Part Three: An incorrect label

Here are some words and expressions from Part Three of the interview.

*He was a **dunce**:* very stupid person

*a career **and stuff**:* and other related things (slang)

*He adopted that **label**:* identity; description of oneself (usually negative)

***It must be true!**:* The speaker is joking here. She doesn't believe what she is saying. (This is an example of sarcasm.)

***What else is there to say?**:* No one could possibly disagree. (This is also said sarcastically.)

*a **menial-type** job:* not requiring much skill, and not well paying

*The **determination** was made:* decision; judgment

*in the **genius** category:* person who is extremely intelligent

*He **internalized** [that new label]:* believed in completely; accepted as true for him

🎧 *Retelling*

One way to make certain that you have understood what you have heard is to retell the information to the speaker or to another listener. You do not need to use the same words.

1➤ Read the following general questions before you listen to Part Three.

1 What happened to the man in Ruth's story when he was in school?

2 What happened to him later in life?

3 What does Ruth find fascinating about this story?

2➤ Now listen to Part Three of the interview. 📼

3➤ Reconstruct Ruth's story with a partner. Tell your partner part of the story, and then let him or her continue. Include answers to the three questions in Step 1.

AFTER THE INTERVIEW

Summarizing what you have heard

1➤ Complete the following summary based on the interview. Use your own words.

Ruth did very _____ in all her school subjects until she encountered _____ in _____ . She didn't _____ , and she didn't know how to _____ because this was the first time that she _____ _____ . Surprisingly, in college Ruth had many _____ , and she really enjoyed _____ , but even though she was good at _____ , she was not good at _____ . Ruth believes that she _____ herself in junior high school as a person who _____ .

Ruth read about a _____ who had done the same thing, based on the results of _____ in high school. The man was labeled a _____ . He believed the label, and after high school he _____ . Years later, he took another test that showed _____ . When the man heard this, he _____ .

2➤ Compare summaries with a partner.

Considering related information: Correlation

Correlation is a statistical measure that tells us how closely related two kinds of information are. For example, if we know someone's IQ, how well can we predict what kind of a student he or she will be, or how good a job he or she will get? A correlation of 1.00 would mean that we can predict completely. For example, if people's IQ scores ranked them in exactly the same order as their grades in school, the correlation between IQ scores and school grades would be 1.00.

1➤ The tables on the next page contain information on how well IQ test scores correlate with other measures of life success. Work with a partner. One of you should look *only* at Table A, and the other *only* at Table B. Ask your partner questions about the missing information in your table, and then fill in the blanks.

Table A

IQ × Other Measures	Correlation
IQ × mental retardation	.90
IQ × years of education	___
IQ × grade point average	.50
IQ × level of job	___
IQ × social and economic status	.40
IQ × success at one's job	___
IQ × social status of one's job	.95
IQ × parents' level of education	___

Student A

What's the correlation between IQ and years of education?

Table B

IQ × Other Measures	Correlation
IQ × mental retardation	___
IQ × years of education	.70
IQ × grade point average	___
IQ × level of job	.50
IQ × social and economic status	___
IQ × success at one's job	.20
IQ × social status of one's job	___
IQ × parents' level of education	.50

Student B

What's the correlation between IQ and mental retardation?

2➤ Interpret the data. What do IQ scores tell you? Make as many statements as you can with your partner. Then share them as a class.

A person's IQ score tells you much more about how much education he or she has had than about how successful he or she will be at work.

3   IN YOUR OWN VOICE

In this section you will give your opinions about the value and limits of intelligence testing, and you will interview a teacher.

Sharing your personal and cultural perspective

1▶ Read and think about the following questions. Share your responses with a partner.

1 Ruth and the man in her story both gave themselves labels early in life. Though usually negative, labels can also be positive. In either case, they are powerful. What kind of labels have you given yourself in your life, and why? Have they been helpful or harmful, in your opinion?

2 What labels have been given to you by others? Did they help you or hurt you?

2▶ Read and discuss the following with a group of classmates – if possible, with those from different cultures.

1 Make a list of the various factors that contribute to a person's success in school, work, and life. Decide which of them could be measured by an intelligence test, and which could not.

2 How are IQ tests used in your country, if at all? How should they be used, in your opinion?

3▶ Share answers to the questions in Step 2 as a class.

Gathering data

1▶ Work with a partner. Together, interview a teacher outside of class – preferably one who speaks English. Ask his or her opinion about the value of using standardized tests to measure students' intelligence and abilities. Write your questions first and check them with your classroom teacher. The example questions in the box may help you get started.

What age level do you teach?

Do your students take standardized tests? How often?

What are these tests supposed to measure?

2▶ Take notes and give a brief report to your classmates.

4 ACADEMIC LISTENING AND NOTE TAKING:
Intelligence testing – an introduction

In this section you will hear and take notes on a lecture given by Evan Cheng, a professor of psychology. The title of the lecture is *Intelligence Testing – An Introduction*. Professor Cheng will give a history of intelligence testing, including current developments, and conclude with a discussion of some of the problems involved in measuring intelligence.

BEFORE THE LECTURE

Predicting the content: Writing information questions

> One way to predict the content of a lecture is to ask yourself *wh-* questions based on the lecture title or description, and try to answer as many of the questions as you can. Your answers may not all be complete or correct, but the process will help you to focus better on the lecture content.

1➤ Reread the title and description of the lecture at the top of the page.

2➤ Try to imagine what information the lecture will include. Then, on your own paper, write five or six *wh-* questions (*what? when? where? why? how? who?*) about the lecture.

When did people start measuring intelligence?

3➤ Ask a partner your questions, and try to answer your partner's questions.

🎧 *Note taking: Recognizing examples*

> When a lecturer is explaining a point or a new idea, he or she will often include specific examples to make the point clearer. It is important to listen carefully to examples because they can help you to understand what the lecturer means. Including these examples in your notes will also help you recall the meaning of the main points when you look back at your notes after the lecture.
>
> When you record examples, begin by writing *e.g.* or *ex:* This will make it easier for you to identify them as examples later on. Some examples involve just a few words and are therefore easy to record. Others may be long and complicated. If they are, try to listen for the main idea and then record it briefly using abbreviations and symbols.
>
> How do you know when you are about to hear an example? Listen for expressions like *for example, here's an illustration, such as, say,* or *for instance.*

1➤ The following are one student's notes on five important points from the lecture, *Intelligence Testing – An Introduction*. In the lecture each of these points is followed by an example. Read the notes and be sure that you understand the abbreviated words and symbols.

> 1. Binet made list of important sch. skills, e.g., _____
>
> 2. He age-graded the tasks – e.g., _____
>
> 3. B. figured mental age of normal child, e.g., _____
>
> 4. Definition: ave. child has IQ of 100 – e.g., _____
>
> 5. Kids from poor educ. environ. do badly on trad. IQ tests. ∴ unintelligent?
>   No, e.g., _____

2➤ Now listen to the five excerpts from the lecture. Take notes on the examples given after each point listed in Step 1. If an example is long, write the main idea only.

3➤ Compare notes with a classmate. Together, reconstruct the excerpts from your notes as best you can. Remember, the purpose of an example is simply to help you understand and recall an important point.

LECTURE, Part One: A history of intelligence testing

Guessing vocabulary from context

1➤ The following items contain some important vocabulary from Part One of the lecture. Each of the vocabulary terms is printed in **boldface** and given in the context in which it occurs. Use the context to help you find the correct definitions on the right. Write the letters in the blanks. Check your guesses in a dictionary if necessary.

_____ *1* How did Binet go about trying to **devise** his test?	*a* mathematical relation between two different things
_____ *2* a **premise**, or a theory on which to base the test	*b* intelligent
	c not intelligent
_____ *3* a huge **assortment** of tasks	*d* increasingly over time
_____ *4* The tasks get **progressively** more difficult.	*e* present; happening today
_____ *5* The seven-year-old was very **bright**.	*f* mathematical statement of a rule
_____ *6* We would say that the five-year-old was **dull** and would have some learning problems.	*g* create; make
	h idea with which you begin research
_____ *7* a **ratio** measure of intelligence	*i* collection; variety
_____ *8* By this **formula**, an average child has an IQ of 100.	
_____ *9* our **current** usage of IQ tests	

2➤ Compare matches with a partner.

🎧 Outlining practice

1➤ The following is an incomplete outline of Part One of the lecture. Examine the structure of the outline and try to predict what kind of information you will hear.

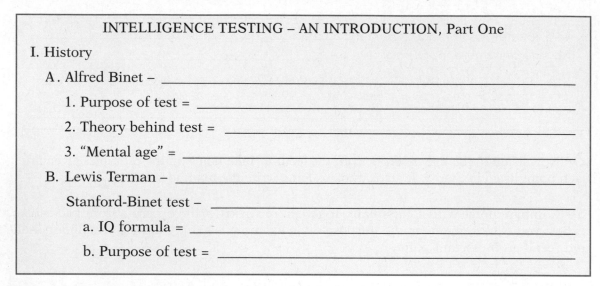

INTELLIGENCE TESTING – AN INTRODUCTION, Part One

I. History

  A. Alfred Binet – _____

     1. Purpose of test = _____

     2. Theory behind test = _____

     3. "Mental age" = _____

  B. Lewis Terman – _____

     Stanford-Binet test – _____

      a. IQ formula = _____

      b. Purpose of test = _____

2➤ Now listen to Part One of the lecture. Take notes on your own paper. 📼

3➤ Use your notes to complete the outline. You do not need to include everything that you heard; just fill in the blanks.

4➤ Compare outlines with a partner. They do not have to be exactly the same.

LECTURE, Part Two: Current approaches and some problems

Guessing vocabulary from context

1➤ The following items contain some important vocabulary from Part Two of the lecture. Use the context to help you choose the definitions on the right. Write the letters in the blanks. Check your guesses in a dictionary if necessary.

_____ 1 The test takes a long time to **administer**.

_____ 2 putting together puzzles and other **visual-spatial skills**

_____ 3 not related to life success in any **significant** way

_____ 4 a very strong culture **bias**

_____ 5 have a hard time surviving in a **rough** neighborhood

_____ 6 You need **"street smarts"** in order to get along.

_____ 7 to survive and **thrive** in that situation

a grow and develop well

b ability to see and work with objects and shapes

c poor and dangerous

d intelligence developed in everyday situations

e unfair advantage or preference

f give (as a test)

g important; noticeable

2▸ Compare matches with a partner.

🎧 *Outlining practice*

1▸ The following is an incomplete outline of Part Two of the lecture. Examine the structure of the outline and try to predict what kind of information you will hear.

INTELLIGENCE TESTING – AN INTRODUCTION, Part Two

II. Current approaches to intelligence assessment

   A. Wechsler Scales = _____

     Different from Stanford-Binet:

      1. _____

      2. _____

III. _____

   A. Definition: _____

   B. Bias: _____

      _____

2▸ Now listen to Part Two of the lecture. Take notes on your own paper. 📼

3▸ Use your notes to complete the outline. You do not need to include everything that you heard.

4▸ Compare outlines with a partner. They do not have to be exactly the same.

AFTER THE LECTURE

Sharing your personal and cultural perspective

Discuss the following questions with a classmate or in a small group.

1 Binet's test was designed to identify "dull" children. Do you think children should be told that they're bright or dull? Why or why not?

2 Do you know anybody who is very intelligent in some ways but not in others?

3 Remember what the lecturer said about "street smarts." Do you have a term for this in your language? Give an example of "street smarts" from your culture.

CHAPTER 6

Accounting for Variations in Intelligence

1 GETTING STARTED

In this section, you will discuss what factors influence intelligence, and you will hear information about test scores on the Scholastic Achievement Test (SAT), which is taken every year by U.S. high school seniors.

Reading and thinking about the topic

1➤ Read the following passage.

> However we define intelligence, it is clear that some of this mysterious quality is inherited from our parents (*nature*), and some of it is the result of how we are brought up (*nurture*). But which has the greater influence? Researchers have been debating this question for years, and there are scientific studies to support both the nature and the nurture sides of the argument.
>
> One of the most controversial questions in the nature/nurture debate concerns gender and IQ: Is there a biological difference in IQ between men and women? Is one sex "smarter"? The latest research seems to say no. It is true that there *are* some differences in how well males and females perform on certain mental tasks. However, on general IQ tests, we find no measurable differences between the sexes.

2➤ Answer the following questions according to the information in the passage.

1 What does *nature* mean? What about *nurture*?

2 What does research on intelligence say about the role of nature versus that of nurture?

3 According to the most recent research, is there a difference in intelligence between the sexes?

3➤ Discuss your own experiences and opinions with a partner.

1 Can you think of any examples to show that nature affects intelligence?

2 What evidence can you give from your own experience to show the importance of nurture in the development of intelligence?

🎧 *Recording numbers*

1➤ You will hear men's and women's average SAT scores for 1972–1996. Before you listen, make some predictions.

1 Who do you think did better on the verbal test – males or females?

2 Who do you think did better on the math test – males or females?

2➤ Listen to the tape and follow the speaker's directions. 📼

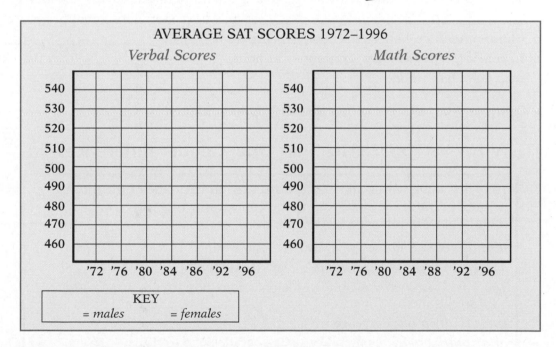

AVERAGE SAT SCORES 1972–1996

Verbal Scores   *Math Scores*

KEY
= males   = females

3➤ Work with a partner and answer the following questions.

1 Compare your dots. Are they the same? Check with other classmates if necessary.

2 Draw lines to connect the dots, then look back at your answers in Step 1. Were you right?

3 Do these results surprise you? Why?

2   AMERICAN VOICES: Dennis

In this section you will hear a three-part interview with Dennis, a public school educator who works with children of elementary and junior high school age. He will discuss differences in how boys and girls perform in school, as well as factors that affect their performance.

BEFORE THE INTERVIEW
Predicting the content

1➤ Use your own knowledge to predict what you will hear about girls' and boys' academic performance in the United States. Complete the following statements. Guess if you're not sure. There may be several possible answers.

1 At about the age of fourteen, boys start to do _____ than girls in math.
2 _____ develop language skills earlier than _____ .
3 One of the reasons why girls start to do _____ in school is that they become more interested in _____ .
4 Boys and girls have different ways of getting attention in class. Girls generally _____ , while boys start acting inappropriately.
5 Children tend do better in school if their parents _____ .
6 In general, kids who have computers at home _____ than kids who don't have them.

2➤ Compare your answers with a partner. Discuss differences.

INTERVIEW WITH DENNIS, Part One: Gender differences

> Here are some words and expressions used in Part One of the interview, printed in **boldface** and given in the context in which you will hear them. They are followed by definitions.
>
> *middle school:* grades six through eight or nine
> *an elementary school **principal**:* head of a school
> *That's become **a cliché**:* an idea that everyone has already heard; old information
> *tends to **drop off**:* decrease
> *in **primary** grades:* elementary, usually grades one to three
> ***acquisition** of language:* learning
> ***fine motor skills**:* skill in printing, drawing, using small tools
> *boys start **asserting themselves**:* speaking out; expressing opinions
> ***slightly inappropriate**:* a little bit rude; not completely acceptable
> *They **"dumb down"**:* act less intelligent than they are

🎧 Listening for specific information

1▸ Read the following incomplete statements before you listen to Part One of the interview. Try to predict what kind of information you will need to complete them.

Dennis

  1 Dennis has been working in public schools for _____ years.

  2 He has done most of his teaching at the _____ level.

  3 Girls do better in the first years of school because they acquire _____ and fine motor skills _____ boys, and they generally _____.

  4 When they want to get the teacher's attention in class, boys are more likely to _____, while girls generally _____ or _____.

  5 Girls start to "dumb down" in middle school because _____.

2▸ Now listen to Part One of the interview. Complete the statements in Step 1. 📼

3▸ Compare answers with a partner. They do not have to be exactly the same.

INTERVIEW WITH DENNIS, Part Two: Different expectations

> Here are some words and expressions from Part Two of the interview.
>
> *how a question is* **assigned**: asked of a specific student
> **cognitive** *research people*: concerning how we think, how our brains work
> *this* **rapid-fire** *question-answer pattern*: very fast
> *someone you don't* **anticipate is going to be** *very successful*: expect to be
> **questioning strategy**: method or style of asking questions
> **puts** *girls* **at a disadvantage**: makes it harder for (girls)

🎧 Listening for specific information

1▸ Read the following statements before you listen to Part Two. Think about what kind of information you will need to complete them.

  1 According to cognitive research, when a teacher asks a question very quickly, the student being questioned _____.

  2 Research shows that when traditional high school math teachers ask questions, they tend to _____.

  3 Researchers believe that math teachers do this because _____ _____.

2➤ Now listen to Part Two of the interview. Complete the statements in Step 1. 🔲

3➤ Compare answers with a partner. They do not have to be exactly the same.

INTERVIEW WITH DENNIS, Part Three: Factors affecting school performance

Here are some words and expressions from Part Three of the interview.

*a very **wealthy** neighborhood*: rich; having a lot of money

low-income housing: government-supported homes for people with low incomes

*I saw a wide **range***: variety of different cases, from one extreme to the other

***access to** computers*: having (computers) available

*can really **turn out** outstanding work*: produce; create

outstanding: of very high quality; excellent

*The content has improved, too, not just the **presentation***: how something looks on paper

*The differences **compound** with each generation*: multiply; get bigger

*just totally **blow it***: do very badly (slang)

*totally **out of control***: behaving very badly

***kinesthetic** intelligence*: related to body movement and muscle control

*They **perceive** the information*: understand; grasp

*able to **replicate** these movements*: imitate; copy

*kids who really **excel** at that*: do excellently

🎧 Listening for specific information

1➤ Read the following statements before you listen to Part Three. Think about what kind of information you will need to complete them.

1 Dennis has observed that in general, if parents have money and think that education is important, their children _____ in school.

2 Dennis taught at a school where the students came from very _____ backgrounds.

3 Dennis believes that having a computer at home _____ .

4 According to Dennis, not all low-income children do _____ in school, and not all wealthy _____ .

5 Dennis cites siblings with similar skills at basketball as evidence to support the idea that _____ intelligence is _____ .

2➤ Now listen to Part Three of the interview. Complete the statements in Step 1. 🔲

3➤ Compare answers with a partner. They do not have to be exactly the same.

4➤ Look back at your answers to *Predicting the content* on page 74. How many statements did you complete correctly?

Kinesthetic intelligence on the basketball court

AFTER THE INTERVIEW

Applying general concepts to specific data

1➤ The following are five factors that Dennis mentioned as influences on a child's performance in school. Read them and decide whether each one is hereditary (*nature*) or environmental (*nurture*). Write *H* for Hereditary or *E* for Environmental.

_____ *1* Girls' desire to attract boys   _____ *4* Earlier acquisition of language

_____ *2* Kinesthetic intelligence   _____ *5* Parents who value education

_____ *3* Access to computers

2➤ Compare answers as a class. Discuss any differences you have.

3➤ For each factor in Step 1, write a true statement based on what you heard in the interview. You can change the wording in the phrases to fit your statements.

> 5. A child is likely to do well in school if his or her parents think education is important.

4➤ Read your statements to a partner, and see if you agree with each other. It's okay if you don't agree! Support your opinions.

Comparing information from different sources

1➤ Read the following excerpt from an article about the SAT.

> The SAT is supposed to predict only how well students will do in their first year of college. But despite lower SAT scores among girls, they consistently receive higher grades than boys in all subjects in their first year of college. ... SAT spokespeople say the differences in scores result chiefly from the fact that boys take more calculus, computer sciences, and lab science. Mrs. Wolfe, a critic of the test and president of the Center for Women Policy Studies, said that boys and girls score differently because of their approach to taking tests. Girls tend to work out math problems, she said, while boys employ "test-taking tricks," like plugging in the answers already offered in a multiple-choice question. While girls are deliberate, "boys play this test like a pin-ball machine."

2▶ Discuss the following questions with one or two classmates.

1 We have already seen in Section 1 of this chapter that males do better on the SAT. What may be the reason, according to the article?

2 Can you see any connection between what Dennis said about boys' classroom behavior and what the article says about their test-taking strategies?

3 Can you think of any other reasons to explain why women get higher grades in college than men?

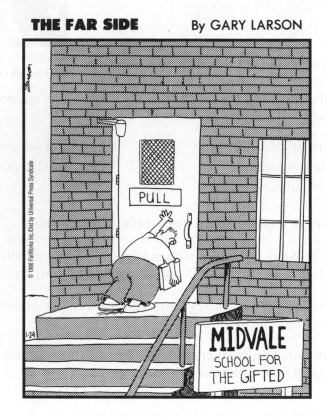

THE FAR SIDE   By GARY LARSON

PULL

MIDVALE
SCHOOL FOR
THE GIFTED

3   IN YOUR OWN VOICE

In this section you will express your own views on factors affecting school performance, and you will have a chance to talk about an aspect of your own intelligence.

Sharing your personal and cultural perspective

Read and think about the following questions. Then discuss them in a small group.

1➤ Obviously, there is a difference between intelligence and performance. For various reasons, some very intelligent students do not perform well in school. What environmental factors can prevent a child from performing up to the level of his or her intelligence?

2➤ What can a teacher do to help students work up to their potential?

3➤ Some of the factors affecting school performance that Dennis described may not exist in schools in your culture (which is, after all, a different environment). For example, do teachers in your culture ask questions in the rapid way that Dennis describes? Talk to a partner (if possible, someone from another culture) about the factors that influence the academic performance of girls and boys in your country.

Giving an oral presentation

In his interview Dennis mentioned Harvard psychologist Howard Gardner's theory of multiple intelligences. Gardner proposes that there are different kinds of intelligence, including *kinesthetic*, *musical*, *spatial*, *logical-mathematical*, and *interpersonal* intelligence.

1➤ Think of a natural ability that you have – something that you do well. It may be solving word puzzles, or drawing, or making something with your hands, or listening to your friends' problems. Also think about whether you inherited this ability from a parent or grandparent (nature), or got interested in it because of someone you know (nurture), or perhaps both.

2➤ Prepare a short presentation about your ability. Tell your classmates when and how you got interested in doing it, how you developed your ability, and what you enjoy about it. Demonstrate if possible.

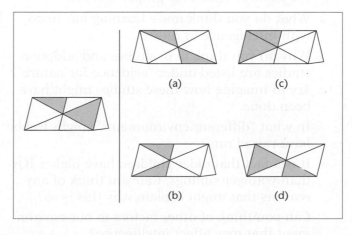

Spatial puzzle: The figure on the left is rotated. Which of the four figures on the right is the same as the one on the left?

4 ACADEMIC LISTENING AND NOTE TAKING: Intelligence – nature or nurture?

In this section you will hear and take notes on a two-part lecture given by Ellen Cash, professor of psychology. The title of the lecture is *Intelligence – Nature or Nurture?* Professor Cash will present evidence to support both the nature and nurture arguments for the development of intelligence.

BEFORE THE LECTURE

Predicting the content

1➤ Read Professor Cash's lecture notes.

> *Week 7 Lecture*
>
> Intelligence – nature or nurture?
>   Evidence for nature
>   • Tryon: rats and maze learning
>   • human twin studies
>   • adoption studies
>   Evidence for nurture
>   • Hebbe: rats raised in different environments
>   • human studies: effect of children's environment
>   • Zajonc: confluence model – why older siblings have higher IQs
>   • other factors to be researched

2➤ Discuss the following questions with a partner.

1 What research scientists will be mentioned in the lecture? (Look for proper names.)

2 What do you think maze learning has to do with intelligence in rats?

3 Why do you think twin studies and adoption studies are listed under "evidence for nature"? Try to imagine how these studies might have been done.

4 In what "different environments" might Hebbe have raised rats?

5 It is a fact that older children have higher IQs than younger siblings. Can you think of any reasons that might explain why this is so?

6 Can you think of other factors in our environment that may affect intelligence?

Laboratory rats in a maze

🎧 Note taking: Recording numbers

> When a lecturer mentions a number or a name, you should write it down. Numbers are not as difficult to write as names because they do not present a spelling problem. However, a number by itself is meaningless: You also need to note what the unit of measure is. Is it a year? a correlation? a dollar amount? a percentage? If it is a percentage, what is it a percentage *of*? If it is a year, what happened in that year?

1➤ Read the following descriptions. Each of them identifies a number that you will hear in taped excerpts from the lecture. (Review the task *Considering related information: Correlation* on page 65, for an explanation of the term *correlation*.)

a _____ = correlation of IQs found in identical twins raised together

b _____ = correlation of IQs found in identical twins raised apart

c _____ = correlation of IQs found in fraternal twins raised together

d _____ = correlation of IQs found in siblings raised together

e _____ = average increase in IQ of children taken from a poor inner-city environment and raised in middle-class homes

f _____ = what the IQ correlation between identical twins would be if heredity were the only factor determining IQ

g _____ = when William Tryon did his work with rats

2➤ Now listen to the excerpts from the lecture. When you hear a number, write it in the correct space in Step 1. Include the unit of measure if you hear one. 📼

3➤ Compare numbers with a classmate. Discuss what each of these numbers means.

LECTURE, Part One: Evidence for the role of nature

Guessing vocabulary from context

1➤ The following nine items contain some important vocabulary from Part One of the lecture. Each of the terms is printed in **boldface** in the context in which you will hear it. Work with a partner. Using context, take turns trying to guess the meanings.

_____ 1 What **determines** intelligence?

_____ 2 One of the big **debates** among researchers is, "Is intelligence something that is inherited?"

_____ 3 difficult to determine the **relative** influence of nature and nurture

_____ 4 He had rats run through a **maze**.

_____ 5 He had these rats **breed** separately and found that after a few generations the bright rats were producing bright babies.

_____ 6 There's a significant **genetic** influence on intelligence.

_____ 7 **Identical** twins share exactly the same DNA.

_____ 8 Identical twins share exactly the same **DNA**.

_____ 9 **Fraternal** twins in terms of DNA are like regular siblings.

2► Match the terms in Step 1 with their definitions by writing the letters in the blanks. Note that the definitions reflect the way in which the terms are used in the lecture; some of these terms can have different meanings in other contexts.

Courtney and Chris Salthouse of Chamblee, Georgia, were the first twins in history to score 1600 on the SAT at the same time.

a caused by heredity

b causes; explains

c formed from two fertilized eggs

d material that determines heredity

e arguments

f system of confusing paths in which one can easily get lost

g comparative; considered in relation to something else

h have children

i formed from one egg that divides into two

🎧 Listening for specific information

1► Read over the following questions on Part One of the lecture. Think about what kind of information you will need to answer them.

INTELLIGENCE – NATURE OR NURTURE? Part One

1 Is there a clear answer to the question of what determines intelligence? Explain.

2 What animal research is there to support the "nature" view of intelligence?

3 Why do identical twins raised together have more similar IQ scores than fraternal twins raised together?

4 Why do fraternal twins have more similar IQ scores than siblings of different ages?

5 What is there in the research on identical twins which shows us that nature is not the only factor determining intelligence?

6 How do adoption studies support the nature view?

2► Now listen to Part One of the lecture. Take notes on your own paper. Use the questions in Step 1 as a guide to help you listen for the important points. 📼

3► Use your notes to answer the questions in Step 1. You may write your answers on paper or answer the questions orally with a partner. Answer as fully as possible.

LECTURE, Part Two: Evidence for the role of nurture

Guessing vocabulary from context

1➤ The following items contain some important vocabulary from Part Two of the lecture. Work with a partner. Using context, take turns trying to guess the meanings.

_____ *1* He raised them in an **enriched** environment – lots of things to do.

_____ *2* raised in an **impoverished** environment – nothing to do

_____ *3* formed by the intellectual **climate** in which the child is raised

_____ *4* The average IQ gets lower with each **successive** child.

_____ *5* decrease in **funding** for schools

_____ *6* We don't know the effects of two-career families and **day care**.

2➤ Match the vocabulary terms with their definitions by writing the letters in the blanks.

a atmosphere
b following
c money used for a specific purpose
d without many things to stimulate the brain
e interesting; stimulating
f system where people are paid to watch children while their parents are working

3➤ Compare matches with a partner.

Listening for specific information

1➤ Read over the following questions on Part Two of the lecture. Think about what kind of information you will need to answer them.

INTELLIGENCE – NATURE OR NURTURE? Part Two

1 Explain Hebbe's experiment with rats and state why it supports the nurture view of intelligence.

2 How does a child's environment affect his or her intellectual development, according to the studies cited in the lecture?

3 Who developed the confluence model, and what is it supposed to account for?

4 Explain the confluence model briefly.

5 The lecture mentioned several other environmental factors that could affect a child's intellectual development. Name as many as you can.

2➤ Now listen to Part Two of the lecture. Take notes on your own paper. Use the questions in Step 1 as a guide to help you listen for the important points. 🎞️

3▶ Use your notes to answer the questions in Step 1. You may write your answers or answer orally with a partner. Answer as completely as you can.

AFTER THE LECTURE

Sharing your personal and cultural perspective

1▶ Discuss the following questions with a partner.

1 Go over the environmental factors mentioned at the end of the lecture (TV viewing, etc.). How would you expect each to influence intellectual development, if at all?

2 Can you think of other environmental factors that might affect a person's intellectual development?

2▶ Read the following excerpt from an article about the twins who both scored 1600 on the SAT (see photo on page 82). Discuss the questions with a partner.

> Mrs. Salthouse, a homemaker who volunteers at the twins' school, said that her children . . . had not been exceptionally early readers. . . . She said her approach, and that of her husband Timothy, a psychology professor, . . . was to let them learn at their own pace, read a lot, and pursue their own interests. "I know I've seen kids pushed too hard, and it bothered me," Mrs. Salthouse said. "I just wanted to make sure a lot was available to them, so they could take advantage of it."

Do you agree with Mrs. Salthouse's ideas about raising intelligent children? In your culture, how do parents nurture their children intellectually? Who generally has more influence on children's intellectual development – their mother or their father? What about in your own family?

Thinking critically about the topic

> **Y**ou will not always agree with what you read or hear. Make it a habit to evaluate what other people say in light of your own knowledge and experiences.

Discuss the following questions with a partner or in a small group.

1 Robert Zajonc's confluence model says that young children lower the average IQ of the family. Does his theory make sense to you?

2 If Zajonc's theory is true, what would we expect to find in an extended family?

3 In your personal experience, are eldest children more intelligent than their brothers and sisters? Are they different in other ways?

UNIT 4

Nonverbal Messages

I n this unit you will hear people discuss nonverbal communication. Chapter 7 deals with *body language*. You will hear interviews with three immigrants to the United States, as well as a lecture on body language across cultures. Chapter 8 covers how we communicate via *touch*, *space*, and *artifacts* (e.g., clothing, jewelry, and furniture). The same three immigrants will discuss cultural differences they have noticed in these channels of communication. Finally, you will hear a lecture on three different aspects of nonverbal communication.

85

CHAPTER 7

Body Language

1 GETTING STARTED

In this section you will discuss the different aspects of body language and identify some common gestures used in the United States.

Reading and thinking about the topic

1➤ Read the following passage.

> Humans use language to communicate, but we also communicate *nonverbally* with our bodies. The way in which we stand or sit, how we use our eyes, what we do with our hands, as well as what we wear – all of these convey powerful messages to other people. In fact, anthropologists claim that only a small percentage of what we communicate is verbal; most of it is nonverbal.
>
> Some of our body language is conscious, such as the "thumbs up" gesture used in many cultures to signal "OK." But much of what we communicate with our bodies is unconscious. Even in one's own culture, unconscious body language can be difficult to read. Imagine, then, how much more incomprehensible the body language of someone from a different culture would be!

2➤ Answer the following questions according to the information in the passage.

  1 With what parts of our bodies do we convey nonverbal messages?
  2 What is conscious body language? Give an example.
  3 What is unconscious body language? Think of an example.

3➤ Discuss your experiences with a partner.

1 Think of examples of conscious body language used in your culture. Demonstrate them and explain what they mean.

2 Have you ever misunderstood the body language of someone from a different culture? Explain.

🎧 *Reading nonverbal cues*

> **A**lways pay attention to nonverbal cues like gestures and head movements. They are a very important dimension of communication.

1➤ Look at the gestures in the drawings. What message do you think each person is communicating? Discuss your guesses with a classmate.

2➤ Listen to the tape and follow the speaker's directions. 📼

a _____ b _____ c _____ d _____ e _____ f _____ g _____ h _____

3➤ Compare matches as a class. Did you get the same answers?

4➤ Take a class survey. Do you think the gestures shown in the drawings are universal? Or do some of them mean something different in different cultures?

2 AMERICAN VOICES: Marcos, SunRan, and Airi

In this section you will hear interviews with three immigrants to the United States: Marcos, SunRan, and Airi. They come from Brazil, Korea, and Japan, respectively. They will talk about differences that they have noticed in American gestures, facial expressions, and eye contact.

BEFORE THE INTERVIEWS

Recalling what you already know

1➤ Think about the body language of people in your country. How much use do they make of eye contact, gestures, and facial expressions? Compare this with what you know or think about body language in other cultures.

2➤ Complete the chart by circling a number from 1–5. A number *1* means a little body language, and a number *5* means a lot. Don't worry if you're not sure; just make your best guess. If you are from Japan, Korea, or Brazil, leave the first line blank.

NONVERBAL COMMUNICATION: Use of body language				
	A little	*An average amount*		*A lot*
People in my country use . . .	1	2	3	4	5
I think Americans use . . .	1	2	3	4	5
I think Japanese use . . .	1	2	3	4	5
I think Koreans use . . .	1	2	3	4	5
I think Brazilians use . . .	1	2	3	4	5

3➤ Compare guesses with a partner. Discuss differences.

INTERVIEW WITH MARCOS: Brazilian body language

> Here are some words and expressions used in the interview, printed in **boldface** and in the context in which you will hear them. They are followed by definitions.
>
> *I wanted* ***to pick your brain****:* to get some information from you (informal)
> *My eyes tend* ***to wander****:* to move around, to look in different directions
> *They* ***talk with their hands****:* use hand gestures as they are speaking
> *Brazilians* ***indeed*** *talk a lot with their hands:* truly; in fact
> *because of an* ***unfamiliar*** *gesture:* unknown; not recognized
> ***I wasn't doing any such thing!****:* You're wrong! I was not doing that.

🎧 Answering true/false questions

1➤ Read these statements before you listen to the interview with Marcos.

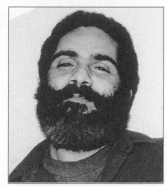

_____ 1 Marcos has lived in the United States since 1981.

_____ 2 According to Marcos, North Americans use more eye contact than Brazilians.

_____ 3 Marcos tends to look all around him when he's listening to someone.

_____ 4 Marcos noticed that his Spanish relatives talked a lot with their hands.

_____ 5 Marcos says that people in the United States use their hands much less than Brazilians do.

_____ 6 Marcos' North American wife was confused by the way Marcos waved to her.

Marcos

2➤ Now listen to the interview. Mark the statements *T* (true) or *F* (false).

3➤ Compare answers with a partner. Correct the false statements together.

INTERVIEW WITH SUNRAN: Korean body language

> Here are some words and expressions from the interview.
>
> *American* **hand signals**: hand movements that have a specific meaning
> *the way you say "come," with your* **palm** *upward*: the inside part of the hand
> *their middle finger instead of their* **index finger**: finger next to the thumb
> **I bet!**: I understand what you mean! (informal)
> *It means they are* **interested**: physically attracted
> *It meant you were* **bad-mannered**: not polite; improper
> *I try to* **minimize** *that*: reduce; do less
> **How come** *you move so much?*: why (informal)
> *How come you don't* **sit still**?: sit quietly without moving

🎧 Answering true/false questions

1➤ Read the following statements before you listen to the interview with SunRan.

_____ 1 SunRan has lived in the United States since she was ten years old.

_____ 2 In Korea, the American gesture for "come here" is used to call dogs.

_____ 3 Older Koreans sometimes point with their little finger – a gesture that has a rude meaning in the United States.

_____ 4 When talking to an older person or someone with a higher social position, Koreans traditionally look at the person's feet.

_____ 5 Between males and females, direct eye contact is a sign of attraction.

_____ 6 After ten years in the United States, SunRan's body language is still completely Korean.

2► Now listen to the interview. Mark the statements *T* (true) or *F* (false). ⊏▭⊐

3► Compare answers with a partner. Correct the false statements together.

INTERVIEW WITH AIRI: Japanese body language

> Here are some words and expressions from the interview.
>
> *a **formal picture**:* posed photograph for a special occasion like a marriage or graduation
>
> ***moving your hand to show "so-so, sort of"**:* See *Reading nonverbal cues,* drawing 8 (page 87).
>
> *more than is **typical**:* usual; common
>
> *I started **dating** my husband:* going out with; seeing socially

⌒ *Restating what you have heard*

1► Read the incomplete paragraphs and try to predict how you might fill in the blanks.

> Airi is married to_____, and she has lived in the United States for_____. Airi discovered one difference in body language between Americans and _____ when she saw herself in a _____ taken at her _____ wedding. All of the people in the picture were _____ with their _____ showing – except for _____. She felt _____ when she saw the picture.
>
>   Airi thinks that Japanese and Americans have similar attitudes about eye contact: In both countries, it's good for people to _____ when they're talking because it shows that they _____ .
>
>   Airi has noticed that Americans use more _____ than Japanese. However, Airi says that she is more like an American in this respect: She started using a lot of _____ when she met _____ because it was so difficult to _____ .

2► Now listen to the interview, and then complete the paragraphs. ⊏▭⊐

3► Compare paragraphs with a classmate. They do not have to be exactly the same.

AFTER THE INTERVIEWS

Thinking critically about the topic

> **D**on't forget to evaluate the opinions of others in light of your own knowledge and experience. The ability to think critically is one of the most important skills for a student to develop.

We can make generalizations about body language, but it is important to remember two things:

- Body language is very complex and largely unconscious.
- Everyone's experience is different.

Read and think about the following questions, and then discuss them as a class.

1 In this section you heard some generalizations about body language in the United States. From your experience and knowledge, do you agree or disagree with what was said?

2 SunRan and Airi have felt the influence of American body language. Whether or not you have spent time in the United States, has your body language been influenced by American culture? If so, how?

3 What generalizations can you make about body language in your culture? If you are from Japan, Korea, or Brazil, do you disagree with anything you heard in the interviews? Can you add more information?

Airi at the wedding of her American sister-in-law

Considering related information

1➤ Read this list of body signals. To make sure you understand them, perform them for a partner.

- scratching the head
- shrugging the shoulders
- lifting an eyebrow
- winking
- tapping the fingers
- leaning forward quickly

2➤ Body signals can have more than one meaning. The sentences in boxes A and B on the next page give two meanings for each of the signals in Step 1. One of you should look *only* at box A, and the other *only* at box B. Ask your partner questions to find the information you need to fill in the blanks in the sentences.

A

1 *Lifting an eyebrow* might mean _____ , or it might mean surprise.

2 *Shrugging the shoulders* might mean the person doesn't care, or it might mean _____ .

3 *Scratching the head* might mean _____ _____ , or it might mean the person has an itch.

4 *Tapping the fingers* might mean impatience, or it might mean _____ .

5 *Winking* might mean _____ , or it might mean the person's not serious.

6 *Leaning forward quickly* might mean forcefulness, or it might mean _____ .

B

1 *Lifting an eyebrow* might mean disbelief, or it might mean _____ .

2 *Shrugging the shoulders* might mean _____ , or it might mean the person doesn't know.

3 *Scratching the head* might mean the person is confused, or it might mean _____ .

4 *Tapping the fingers* might mean _____ , or it might mean anxiety.

5 *Winking* might mean intimacy, or it might mean _____ .

6 *Leaning forward quickly* might mean _____ , or it might mean the person wants attention.

3   IN YOUR OWN VOICE

In this section you will do some research of your own on the subject of body language and then present your results to your classmates.

Gathering data

Do the following on your own.

1➤ Do some field research on body language! Choose an aspect of body language to observe: hand gestures, eye contact, or facial expressions.

2➤ Go to a place where you can watch people without being noticed. Some good places are cafés, shopping malls, parks, and train or bus stations. Make notes as you watch. Pay attention to gender, ethnicity, and age differences, and make guesses about the relationships between the people that you observe. Are they friends? Are they married? What makes you think so? Watch for at least forty-five minutes.

3➤ Analyze your observations and prepare a brief report. Include what aspect of body language you were observing, where you were, how many people you observed, and what conclusions you reached based on your observations.

4➤ Present your report to the class. Take notes as you listen to your classmates' reports.

Asking for clarification

> **A**fter you listen to a lecture or an oral presentation, it is important to check your notes and ask questions right away about anything you missed or did not understand. It may help you to begin with one of these questions:
>
> • What did you mean by _____?
> • I didn't understand what you said about _____.
> • Can you repeat what you said about _____?
> • What does the phrase/term _____ mean?

Work in a small group. Look over the notes you took on the reports given by the members of your group in the previous task, *Gathering data*. Ask each of the people in your group two or three questions about their reports to clarify anything you did not understand.

4   ACADEMIC LISTENING AND NOTE TAKING: Body language across cultures

In this section you will hear and take notes on a two-part lecture given by Ellen Summerfield, a professor of communication arts. The title of the lecture is *Body Language Across Cultures*. Professor Summerfield will discuss the challenges of understanding the nonverbal aspects of communication in a different culture.

BEFORE THE LECTURE

Looking beyond the facts

> **A**lways look beyond the facts that you hear and read, and consider what they mean in concrete terms. One good way to do this is to relate the facts to your own experience.

1➤ Read and think about the following quotations on nonverbal communication.

> "[A]nthropologists claim that only a small percentage of what we communicate is verbal; most of it is nonverbal." – Introductory reading to this chapter, see page 86
>
> "[E]xperts in the field of communication estimate that somewhere between 60 and 90 percent of everything that we communicate is nonverbal." – Professor Ellen Summerfield, *Body Language Across Cultures*

2➤ How can it possibly be true that 60–90 percent of all our communication is nonverbal? With a partner, brainstorm a list of all the nonverbal cues (e.g., our facial expressions) that influence the meaning of our words.

3➤ With your partner, read and perform the following two-line dialogue with as many different interpretations as you can (e.g., impatience, excitement, anger). Use nonverbal cues to convey the different meanings.

   A: Are you ready?
   B: Yes.

4➤ Perform one of your interpretations of the dialogue for your classmates. Ask them what feeling(s) they thought you were communicating, and what nonverbal cues they noticed.

🎧 *Note taking: Mapping*

> **W**hen you are taking notes on a lecture, you want your notes to reflect the organizational structure of the lecture. We have practiced doing this with indenting. Another method of taking notes is called *mapping*. With mapping, you begin with the main idea near the center of your paper and draw lines out to related points. Mapping has several advantages:
>
> • It gives a visual representation of the structure of a lecture and the relationships between the ideas.
> • As you take notes, you can show connections between different parts of the lecture simply by adding lines.
> • Mapping makes it easy for you to go back and add further details at any time during a lecture. This is helpful, because lecturers often skip around as they speak and return to add comments about an earlier point.

1➤ Study the following incomplete "map." It represents an excerpt from Professor Summerfield's lecture. There is one main point in the excerpt. How many supporting points are there? How many definitions?

```
                    _____  =  how we hold ourselves
                    _____  =  _____
"body lang."   {    facial expressions
                    _____
                    _____
                    _____
```

2➤ Now listen to the excerpt and complete the map. Listen a second time and fill in anything you missed. 📼

3➤ Compare maps with a partner.

LECTURE, Part One: Aspects of body language

Guessing vocabulary from context

1➤ The following items contain vocabulary from Part One of the lecture. Use the context to help you choose the best definitions. Then check your guesses in a dictionary.

1 We're concerned about how the other person **interprets** our words.
  a changes   *b* disbelieves   *c* understands

2 what we are saying by our **posture**, the way in which we hold ourselves

   a position of our arms   *b* how we sit or stand   *c* our opinion

3 and our **tone of voice**

   a voice quality,   *b* how quickly we speak   *c* pronunciation
     such as loudness

4 Nonverbal communication becomes extremely **complicated**.

   a easy to explain   *b* different   *c* hard to understand

5 After all, if we're learning another language, **what do we learn but words**?

   a We do not learn words. *b* We learn only words.   *c* We learn only gestures.

6 It's very easy to misinterpret these cues, or miss them **altogether**.

   a in a group   *b* completely   *c* unconsciously

7 if you're **puzzled** by what's happening to you in a foreign culture

   a confused   *b* angered   *c* interested

2➤ Compare answers with a partner. Ask your teacher for help if you need to.

🎧 Mapping

1➤ Study the following incomplete map of Part One of the lecture. Try to predict from the map how the lecture is structured.

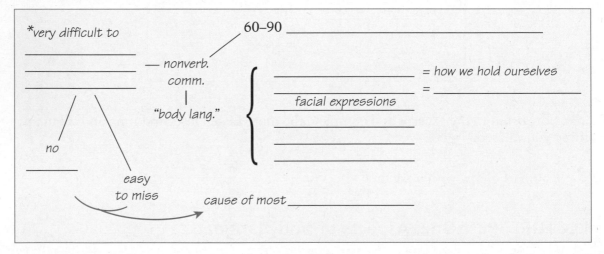

2➤ Now listen to Part One of the lecture. Complete the map as you listen. 📼

3➤ Compare maps with a classmate. They do not have to be exactly the same.

LECTURE, Part Two: Cross-cultural misunderstandings

Guessing vocabulary from context

1► The following items contain some important vocabulary from Part Two of the lecture. Use the context to help you choose the best definitions. Then check your guesses in a dictionary.

1 Looking directly into another person's eyes is **appropriate**, and if you look down, you may be showing disrespect.

    a impolite   *b* proper   *c* friendly

2 I was paying attention to what was said to me rather than to nonverbal **cues**.

    a answers   *b* questions   *c* signs

3 I have great respect for this **colleague**.

    a supervisor   *b* co-worker   *c* employee

4 I know that he wanted to **cooperate**.

    a be helpful   *b* take control   *c* disagree

5 I always interpreted this as a **green light**.

    a warning   *b* signal for "yes"   *c* signal for "no"

6 It's so important if we want to understand the **hidden** side of communication.

    a not obvious   *b* foreign   *c* not polite

2► Compare answers with a partner. Ask your teacher for help if you need to.

🎧 Mapping

1► Study the following incomplete map of Part Two of the lecture. Try to predict from the map how this part of the lecture is structured.

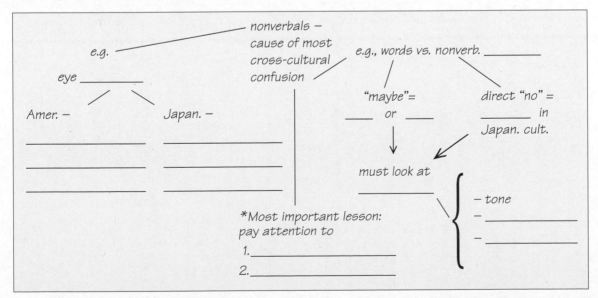

2► Now listen to Part Two of the lecture. Complete the map as you listen. 🔲

3► Compare maps with a partner. They do not have to be exactly the same.

AFTER THE LECTURE

Sharing your personal and cultural perspective

Discuss the following questions with one or two classmates.

  1 You will notice that this chapter contains contradictory information about eye contact in Japan: Airi said that she noticed no big differences between Japanese and American patterns of behavior, but Professor Summerfield said that there is much less direct eye contact in Japan. What does this tell us about the rules of body language?

  2 Think about eye contact in your culture. Are there some situations in which direct eye contact is bad, and others in which it is required? Think of some examples.

  3 Is it sometimes (or always) impolite to say no directly in your culture? Can you think of ways that you express yes or no nonverbally? Compare notes with someone from your culture if possible. Have a short conversation in your own language, and try to pay attention to each other's nonverbal cues.

The Language of Touch, Space, and Artifacts

1 GETTING STARTED

In this section you will hear and discuss how people communicate through touch, space, and artifacts.

Reading and thinking about the topic

1➤ Read the following passage.

> We have seen that nonverbal communication includes use of facial expressions, gestures, and body posture. Two other ways in which we communicate without words are through *touch* and *space*. The cultural rules that control our use of touch (who touches whom? when? where?) and space (how close do we stand to our friends? to strangers?) are very subtle and largely unconscious. In fact, we almost never think about them until they are broken. Then we probably feel very uncomfortable, although we may not know exactly why.
>
> A third way in which we communicate nonverbally is through *artifacts:* What kind of clothing do we wear? What colors? What about jewelry? Hairstyle? Makeup? What kind of car or house do we choose to buy? These choices communicate a lot about how we see ourselves and strongly influence how other people view us.

2➤ Answer the following questions according to the information in the passage.

1 What three types of nonverbal communication will be discussed in this chapter?

2 Give examples of each of the three types.

Chapter 8 The Language of Touch, Space, and Artifacts 99

3➤ Discuss your own experiences and opinions with a partner.

1 Can you think of some examples of cross-cultural differences in the use of touch and space?

2 Choose something that you are wearing right now – something that you bought yourself. It might be a piece of jewelry or an article of clothing. Tell your partner why you chose to buy it and what it says about your character or personality.

Reading nonverbal cues

1➤ The following photographs give examples of nonverbal communication by means of touch, space, and artifacts. As a class, identify which of these three types of nonverbal communication you see in each photograph.

2➤ What seems to be the nonverbal message in each photo? Compare guesses as a class.

1

2

3

4

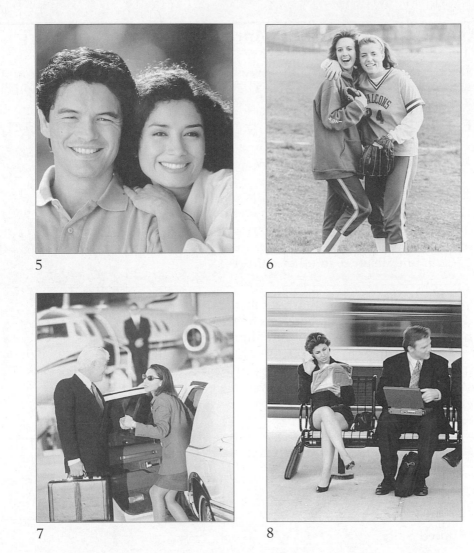

5

6

7

8

🎧 Listening to directions

1➤ Listen to the tape and follow the speaker's directions. 📼

a ____ b ____ c ____ d ____ e ____ f ____ g ____ h ____

2➤ Discuss the following as a class.

1 Compare matches. Do you agree? If not, discuss your differences.

2 The photographs were all taken in the United States. Would the uses of touch, space, and artifacts shown in these photographs have the same meanings in your culture as they do in American culture? If not, what differences would there be?

2   AMERICAN VOICES: Marcos, SunRan, and Airi

In this section you will again hear the three immigrants from Brazil, Korea, and Japan, respectively – Marcos, SunRan, and Airi. They will talk about touch, space, and clothing.

BEFORE THE INTERVIEWS

Recalling what you already know

1➤ Think about the rules of touch and space in your country. How much do people touch one another, and how much distance is there between them when they talk? Compare this with what you know or think about the use of touch and distance in other cultures.

Students in Benin, West Africa

2➤ Complete the following chart about the use of touch and space between males, between females, and between males and females in different cultures. Write numbers *1–3*, according to the key. Don't worry if you're not sure; just make your best guess. If you are from Japan, Korea, or Brazil, leave the first line blank.

NONVERBAL COMMUNICATION: Use of touch and space			
	Between males	*Between females*	*Between males and females*
In my country	____	____	____
In the United States	____	____	____
In Japan	____	____	____
In Korea	____	____	____
In Brazil	____	____	____

KEY

1 = a lot of touch and very little space
2 = average touch and space
3 = very little touch and a lot of space

3➤ Compare and discuss guesses with a partner.

INTERVIEWS WITH MARCOS, SUNRAN, AND AIRI:
Touch and space

Here are some words and expressions used in the interviews, given in the context in which you will hear them. They are followed by definitions.

*He kept **backing up***: moving backward

*this look of total **despair** on his face:* great unhappiness and discomfort

*invaded his **body bubble***: the space around a person that no one should enter

*to **accommodate** us cold North Americans:* make to feel comfortable

***cold** North Americans:* unfriendly; distant

We were much more physical: we touched one another more

*a little **self-conscious***: embarrassed; afraid that other people are watching

You're not supposed to!: shouldn't

*They **hug** and kiss at school:* put their arms around one another

*I felt more **affection** for them:* love; warmth

Summarizing what you have heard

1► Read the following incomplete summaries before you listen to the interviews.

Marcos: Marcos was talking to a _____ of his from _____. After a while he noticed that the student had _____ into a _____ because Marcos kept moving _____ . The student obviously felt very _____ . Marcos had invaded his _____ .

Marcos finds that he and his _____ touch one another _____ here than they did in _____ . Marcos also tries to stand _____ from people now that he lives in the United States.

SunRan: SunRan has learned how to _____ since she came here, but she has to remember _____ when she visits _____ . She says that it is not good for _____ and _____ to _____ in public in her country, but people of the same _____ can hold _____ . However, SunRan has to remember not to do that in the _____ .

When she first came to the United States, SunRan was _____ by the fact that _____ hug and _____ at school.

Airi: Airi says that Japanese people _____ hug and kiss one another. Her American husband felt _____ by this at first: He thought his wife's family didn't _____ When Airi first came to the United States, she was _____ at first because her American family _____ . But now she _____ .

2► Now listen to the interviews, and then complete the summaries.

3► Compare summaries with a partner. They do not have to be exactly the same.

INTERVIEW WITH AIRI: Clothing

> Here are some important words and expressions from the interview.
>
> *casual:* relaxed; comfortable; informal
> *a **status thing***: a question of social position
> *wearing **brand** names:* the manufacturer (e.g., Levi's)
> ***designer labels***: clothing made by famous designers (e.g., Calvin Klein)
> *something that's **in fashion***: popular now
> *a **consultant***: person who is paid to give expert advice or information
> ***kimono***: traditional Japanese robe
> ***cocktail dress***: short formal dress
> ***bridesmaids'*** *dresses:* women (sisters, friends, etc.) in the wedding ceremony

🎧 *Listening for specific information*

1➤ Read the following statements before you listen to the interview. Each statement may be a comment about either Japanese or American people, or it may be about both.

_____ *1* They are casual in the way they dress.

_____ *2* They are concerned about designer labels.

_____ *3* Young people like to wear clothes that are different.

_____ *4* Their clothes say "This is my way."

_____ *5* They want to look the same.

_____ *6* Their weddings are like a fashion show.

_____ *7* They usually plan their own weddings.

2➤ Now listen to the interview. Try to listen for the statements listed in Step 1. Write *J* next to comments about Japanese people, and *A* next to comments about Americans. Write both *J* and *A* if you think a comment is meant to apply to both. 📼

3➤ Compare answers with a partner and then as a class. Discuss differences.

AFTER THE INTERVIEWS

Personalizing the topic

Airi, SunRan, and Marcos all said that their rules for space and touch have changed since they came to the United States. Think about these questions. Share answers as a class.

1 If you are studying in the United States, have your rules for space and touch changed, too? Has your body bubble gotten larger or smaller? Do you touch people more or less than you used to?

2 If you are studying in your own country, have you met foreigners whose use of space and touch were different from yours? What were the differences? How did you or other people react to the differences?

Sharing your cultural perspective

Discuss the following questions with a partner, from another culture if possible.

1 From Airi's perspective, Americans seem very casual in their dress. What is *your* impression of Americans in this respect? How do they compare with people in your culture? Are they more or less formal?

2 Think about other areas of artifactual communication besides those involving clothing – for example, jewelry, cosmetics, cars, or recreational equipment. What messages do typical Americans your age seem to communicate by their choices in these areas? If you are not living in the United States, think about people you have seen in American films or TV programs. For example, what kind of car does an action hero tend to drive, and what message does the car convey?

Considering related information

1➤ Read the following excerpt from an article on touch in *Psychology Today*.

> Touching has a subtle and often ambivalent role in most settings. But there is one special circumstance in which touch is permitted and universally positive: In sports, teammates encourage, applaud, and console one another generously through touch. In Western cultures, for men especially, hugs and slaps on the behind are permitted among athletes, even though they rare among heterosexual men outside the sports arena. . . .
>
> Graduate student Charles Anderton and psychologist Robert Heckel of the University of South Carolina studied touch in the competitive context of all-male or all-female championship swim meets by [counting the number of times that winners and losers were touched]. Regardless of sex, winners were touched . . . on average six times more than losers, with most of the touches to the hand and some to the back or shoulders; only a small percent were to the head or buttocks.

2➤ Answer the following questions with a small group of classmates.

1 According to the article, in what context is touch considered acceptable? Is this true in your culture as well?

2 If you have seen American or European sports events on television, have you noticed how athletes touch one another?

3 According to the article, who is touched more, winners or losers? Why do you think this is so?

3 IN YOUR OWN VOICE

In this section you will do some more research on body language, find and analyze examples of artifactual communication.

Gathering data

1➤ Do some more field research on body language. This time, look for how people use space, touch, or artifacts. If you want to observe people's use of space, watch how they behave in a crowded elevator, or go to a place where people have to stand in line, such as a bank or a movie theater. Cafés or restaurants are a good place to observe touch.

2➤ Take notes on what you see, and remember to record the gender, approximate age, and ethnicity of the people you observe. Also try to determine the relationships between people who seem to be together.

Using examples to illustrate a general point

> Including examples – whether they are stories, statistics, or pictures – is an excellent way of explaining a general point or of making sure that you understand it.

1➤ Work with one or two classmates. Choose one category of artifactual communication. It could be clothing, footwear, hairstyle, makeup, jewelry, color, furniture, cars, architecture, or any other class of artifact that makes a statement about its wearer, owner, or user.

2➤ Look through magazines or newspapers for pictures of your category of artifacts. Discuss what message each picture is trying to convey nonverbally (wealth? sophistication? youth? individualism?). Try to find a variety of messages.

3➤ Cut out your examples and create a collage by pasting them onto a piece of poster board. Number each example in the collage, and write corresponding numbers on a blank sheet of paper, leaving lots of space after each number for your classmates to write in.

4➤ Fasten your poster and sheet of paper to the wall in your classroom, and then walk around and look at the other posters. Use the sheets of paper to write down what you think each example is conveying nonverbally.

5➤ Finally, present your own poster to the class, as a group. Tell what nonverbal message you think each example conveys.

4 ACADEMIC LISTENING AND NOTE TAKING: Nonverbal communication – the hidden dimension of communication

In this section you will hear and take notes on a two-part lecture given by Mara Adelman, a professor of communications. The title of the lecture is *Nonverbal Communication – The Hidden Dimension of Communication*. Professor Adelman will discuss nonverbal communication across cultures, focusing on the areas of humor, space, and touch.

BEFORE THE LECTURE

Recalling what you already know

1► Think of cross-cultural differences that you know about in the three areas that will be covered in the lecture. This may be information from this chapter or from your own experience. Record your ideas in the box.

Humor:
Space:
Touch: Females hold hands in Korea.

2► Share your ideas with a classmate. Did you get any new ideas from each other?

3► Share ideas as a class.

🎧 Note taking: Listening for stress and intonation

> English speakers use stress and intonation when they speak, and these features can be as important to the meaning of a sentence as its grammar or vocabulary. Take, for example, the difference in meaning between "That's my cousin, Bill" (the speaker is talking to Bill about a cousin of the speaker) and "That's my cousin Bill" (the speaker is talking about his cousin who is named Bill). In spoken language, the difference between these two sentences is communicated largely through stress and intonation.
>
> The stress and intonation systems in English are complex, but there are some general patterns that you can start to recognize. In fact, these

Continued . . .

patterns can be especially easy to hear in lectures because lecturers often exaggerate stress and intonation to help students follow what is being said.

Listing   One common pattern is used when a speaker is giving a list. Look at the intonation pattern, indicated with arrows, in this sentence:

This chapter discusses the language of touch, space, and artifacts.

Notice that the speaker's voice rises on each word in the list up until the last one. Then it rises higher and finally falls to a low tone. If it does not fall, the speaker has not finished yet, or has not given a complete list.

Contrast   Another common use of stress and intonation is to show contrast. For example:

Nonverbal communication is difficult enough to understand in one's own

culture, but becomes extremely complicated in another culture.

Here, the speaker is contrasting "own culture" with "another culture" by using raised intonation and added stress, indicated with underlining, on the second syllable of "another."

In general, English speakers use stress and raised intonation to draw the listener's attention to something important. As you begin to notice stress and intonation patterns, you will find that they can help you understand the content of a lecture.

1➤ The following excerpts from the lecture use stress and intonation either to show contrast or to give a list of words. Read them aloud and try to predict what intonation patterns you will hear and what words will be stressed.

1 "How much is conveyed through verbal communication? More often than not, our intense emotions are conveyed nonverbally."

2 "Most of our intense emotions are expressed through gestures, body position, facial expression, vocal cues, eye contact, use of space, and touching."

3 "Imagine what would happen if you don't understand this bubble. What might you experience? Possibly discomfort, irritation, maybe even anger."

4 "It could express affection, anger, playfulness, control, status – these are just a few functions of touch."

5 "In some cultures it is common to see same-sex friends holding hands in public. However, think about this behavior in some other cultures. Is it appropriate?"

2➤ Now listen to the taped excerpts and follow the speaker's directions. Draw arrows to show the intonation that you hear, and underline stressed words or syllables. 📼

3➤ Work with a partner. Compare your marked excerpts. Then try to say each sentence with the stress and intonation patterns that you heard. Discuss what the patterns mean.

LECTURE, Part One: Sarcasm and proxemics

Guessing vocabulary from context

1➤ The following items contain some important vocabulary from Part One of the lecture. Each of the vocabulary terms is printed in **boldface**, in the context in which it occurs. Work with a partner. Using context, take turns trying to guess the meanings.

_____ *1* In humor and **sarcasm**, the verbal message is only a small part of the message.

_____ *2* when Americans go **abroad**

_____ *3* another area that's often **overlooked**

_____ *4* **Proxemics** refers to our personal space.

_____ *5* Body bubbles are very interesting because they're very **subtle**; you hardly ever recognize them.

_____ *6* When someone **violates** your private space, you are suddenly conscious of the bubble.

_____ *7* You might experience **irritation**, even anger.

It is often the nonverbal cues that indicate whether the message is to be taken seriously or not.

2➤ Match the terms in Step 1 with their definitions by writing letters in the blanks. Note that the definitions reflect the way in which the terms are used in the lecture; some of these terms can have different meanings in other contexts.

a to another country
b study of how people communicate through the use of space
c saying the opposite of what one means, often to show annoyance or contempt
d breaks in; enters illegally
e not thought about; forgotten
f mildly upset feeling
g hard to notice

We try to respect the personal space of others.

🎧 Summarizing what you have heard

1> Read the following incomplete summary of Part One of the lecture. Remember that a summary includes only the main points of the lecture and may use different words from those used by the lecturer.

NONVERBAL LANGUAGE – THE HIDDEN DIMENSION OF COMMUNICATION, Part One

Strong emotions are usually conveyed _____: by gestures, body posture, _____ , voice, eye contact, _____ , and _____ .

   Sometimes we rely completely on _____ to communicate. At other times nonverbal cues add to the meaning of the _____ that we use. One good example of the second case is seen in our use of _____ and _____ . Often, in making a joke, Americans will say the opposite of what they mean. The only way to know what they really mean is to _____ the _____ cues that go along with their words. These could be their _____ or a _____ expression.

   An important area of _____ communication is *proxemics*, the study of _____. Each of us has a "_____" around us. Its size depends on several factors, such as _____, the social context, and our _____ . If someone enters our _____, we will _____ . _____ also plays an important role in proxemics; some cultures – for example, _____ – have smaller bubbles than others.

2> Now listen to Part One of the lecture. Take notes on your own paper. Use indenting or mapping – whichever works better for you. 📼

3> Use your notes to complete the summary.

4> Compare summaries with a partner. They do not have to be exactly the same.

LECTURE, Part Two: Touch

Guessing vocabulary from context

1> The following items contain some important vocabulary from Part Two of the lecture. Work with a partner. Using context, take turns trying to guess the meanings.

_____ 1 Touch is one of the most sensitive areas because touch is never **neutral**.

_____ 2 Shaking hands seems almost a **ritual**.

_____ 3 Is it appropriate? Could it be **taboo**?

_____ 4 I decided to **incorporate** the habit when I came back.

_____ 5 We felt very **awkward** about it, and we stopped doing it.

_____ 6 The **norms** for touching are very powerful.

_____ 7 serious misinterpretations or anger or **alienation**

_____ 8 a lot of humor and **camaraderie** between people

2► Match the terms in Step 1 with their definitions by writing the letters in the blanks.

a uncomfortable
b warmth; friendliness
c socially wrong
d start using
e feeling of being an outsider
f social habit, often done without
   much thought
g social rules
h neither positive nor negative

Touch is one of the most sensitive areas of
nonverbal communication.

🎧 Summarizing what you have heard

1► Read the following incomplete summary of Part Two of the lecture.

> **NONVERBAL LANGUAGE – THE HIDDEN DIMENSION**
> **OF COMMUNICATION, Part Two**
>
> Another important form of _____ is _____. As with
> space, rules of _____ are very subtle, and they are mostly determined
> by _____ and _____ . What is acceptable in one culture may be
> _____ in another culture. For example, in China, _____
> _____. But in the United States,
> _____ .
>
>   In conclusion, we should remember that nonverbal _____ do not
> often result in cross-cultural _____ . In fact, these mistakes can be a source
> of _____ and _____ between people of different cultures.

2► Now listen to Part Two of the lecture. Takes notes on your own paper. 📼

3► Use your notes to complete the summary.

4► Compare summaries with a partner. They do not have to be exactly the same.

AFTER THE LECTURE

Sharing your personal and cultural perspective

Discuss the following questions in a small group.

1 Have you had difficulty understanding humor in another language? Talk about why jokes are difficult to understand across cultures. Think of a joke in your language and tell it – in English – to your teacher or to a classmate from a different country if possible. Did the person laugh? Did you need to explain it?

2 When she tried to hold hands with her sister in the United States, the lecturer found that she felt too embarrassed – that cultural norms for touching are too powerful to ignore. If you have ever lived in a foreign country, have you experienced surprise or embarrassment at differences in the norms of touching?

3 Do you have questions about anything that you heard in the lecture? Is there anything that you disagree with? Discuss these points with your group and teacher.

UNIT 5

Interpersonal Relationships

In this unit you will hear men and women talk about the people who are important in their lives. Chapter 9 deals with *friendship*. You will hear an interview with a woman who takes her friendships very seriously, and a lecture on the meaning of friendship. In Chapter 10, on *love*, the author interviews a couple who have been happily married for thirty-three years. The chapter concludes with a lecture on what makes people fall in love with each other.

CHAPTER 9

Friendship

1 GETTING STARTED

In this section you will read and talk about what friendship means, and you will hear six Americans tell when and where they met their best friends.

Reading and thinking about the topic

1➤ Read the following passage.

> Friends play different roles at different times in our lives. We all remember how important it was to have other children to play with when we were young. During the adolescent years, so filled with physical and emotional change, we have more time, more energy, and perhaps a greater need for friendship than we ever will again. As adults, busy with our own lives, we depend less on our friends for support. However, friends still play a critical role for most of us, sharing our happy moments and helping us through difficult times.
>
>   There is a popular rhyme: "Make new friends, but keep the old; one is silver and the other gold." Most of us try to make new friends wherever we go – to a university, to a different job, to a new city – and we usually try to "keep the old" as well. However, maintaining friendships over time and distance is not easy. Americans tend to move around a great deal, and old friendships often suffer as a result.

2➤ Answer the following questions according to the information in the passage.

   1 What different roles does friendship serve to fulfill in childhood, adolescence, and adulthood?

114   *Unit 5 Interpersonal Relationships*

2 Why is friendship especially important during adolescence?

3 Explain the meaning of the rhyme "Make new friends . . . ."

3➤ Discuss your own experiences with a partner.

1 The passage says that Americans often lose touch with old friends. Is this also a problem in your culture, or for you as an individual?

2 Do you have any sayings in your language about the importance of friendship? If so, share them with your class and teacher.

Personalizing the topic

1➤ Work with a partner. First, think of a very good friend of yours. Tell your partner his or her name, and when and where you met. Ask your partner for the same information. Record his or her answers.

My partner's name: _____

His/her good friend's name: _____

When they met: _____

Where they met: _____

2➤ As a class, figure out how long (on average) you and your classmates have known the friends that you named. Where did most of you meet your friends?

🎧 Listening for specific information

1➤ Listen to the tape and follow the speaker's directions. ⌽

SPEAKER	A GOOD FRIEND	WHEN THEY MET	WHERE THEY MET
Otis	Hubert	_____	_____
David	Odette	_____	_____
Pam	Esther	_____	_____
Tony	Tom	_____	_____
Catherine	Douglas	_____	_____
Ruth	Jeanette	_____	_____

2➤ Compare information with a partner. Did you write the same things? Where did most of the speakers meet their friends?

2   AMERICAN VOICES: Catherine

In this section you will hear the author talk to her friend Catherine about Catherine's friendships – how they have started, how she maintains them, and why they are important to her.

BEFORE THE INTERVIEW

Recalling what you already know

1► Complete the following general statements about friendship with your own ideas.

1 Some of the places where people first meet friends are _____

_____ .

2 Friends are important because _____

_____ .

3 In order to keep a friendship strong, you need to _____

_____ .

2► Compare ideas with a partner. Do you agree? Did you get any new ideas?

INTERVIEW WITH CATHERINE, Part One: Starting friendships

Here are some words and expressions used in Part One of the interview, printed in **boldface** and given in the context in which you will hear them. They are followed by definitions.

*What started it was when I **asked you a favor**:* made a request for help

*She had a lot of **fleas**:* very small biting insects that live on animals like dogs and cats

*It seemed fairly **bothersome**:* annoying; troublesome

*I still have the **scars**:* marks that remain after cuts or scratches heal

*My friendships have **sprung from** a shared interest:* grown out of; resulted from

*I have a particular work **ethic**:* a sense of what is right and wrong; rules of behavior

*a course in **linguistics**:* the study of language

*I was so **intimidated** by her coolness:* made to feel afraid or shy

*intimidated by her **coolness**:* quality of being "cool"; good; attractive

*At some point she **revealed** to me:* told something that had been kept secret

*Neither of us was **that cool** after all:* as cool as we had thought before

🎧 Answering true/false questions

1➤ Read the following statements about Part One of the interview. Some are true. Some are false.

_____ 1   Catherine is a teacher.

_____ 2   Catherine met the interviewer because they both had cats.

_____ 3   Catherine has a relaxed attitude about her job.

_____ 4   Catherine met her friend Odette in graduate school.

_____ 5   At first Catherine didn't want to be Odette's friend because Odette wasn't "cool."

Catherine (on right) and a friend

2➤ Now listen to Part One of the interview. Write *T* (true) or *F* (false) next to the statements. Correct the false statements to make them true. 📼

3➤ Compare answers with a partner.

INTERVIEW WITH CATHERINE, Part Two: Maintaining friendships

> Here are some words and expressions from Part Two of the interview.
>
> *I think friendships need **tending**:* care; attention
>
> ***being current** with my friends:* being up to date; knowing what is happening right now
>
> *friends I have **managed to** stay very close to:* succeeded by trying hard
>
> *She's **not much for** writing letters:* doesn't like to; isn't very interested in
>
> *It's a **concrete** record of what we were doing:* real; physical
>
> *didn't know each other **all that well**:* not very well
>
> ***e-mail**:* electronic mail; correspondence by computer
>
> *one friend who just wasn't **into** writing letters:* interested in (slang)
>
> *She **got on line**:* got access to electronic mail
>
> *E-mail is **her thing**:* something that she is very interested in (slang)
>
> *which is **unprecedented**:* completely new; happening for the first time
>
> *I'm **all for** e-mail:* support strongly; am in favor of (informal)
>
> *I want my friends to **call me on** things [that upset them]:* express anger about; object to
>
> *Friendship can get **prickly**:* difficult; uncomfortable
>
> *The other person can **go off into peals of laughter**:* start laughing loudly, uncontrollably
>
> *You've actually **accrued** this common history:* built up; collected over time

🎧 Summarizing what you have heard

1➤ Read the following incomplete summary of Part Two of the interview. Try to predict how you might fill in the blanks.

For Catherine, it's very important to _____ her friends. With some of her friends – for example, Odette – she stays in touch by _____. They talk _____. Catherine also loves to _____, and she never _____. As a result, she has a large collection of _____ that forms a sort of _____ of her life and of her friends' lives. She has been writing to her friend Doug for _____ . With some of her other friends, Catherine stays in touch by _____ .

According to Catherine, one of the most important things that friends can do for each other is _____ . She believes that fighting is a way to show _____ . Other important things that friends give one another are comfort, _____, _____ , and jokes. Finally, Catherine says that _____ are "the family _____ ."

2➤ Now listen to Part Two of the interview. Complete the summary. 📼

3➤ Compare summaries with a classmate. They do not have to be exactly the same.

AFTER THE INTERVIEW

Drawing inferences

Work with a partner. Go back to the task *Recalling what you already know* (in *Before the Interview*) and imagine how Catherine would complete the statements.

Sharing your personal and cultural perspective

Discuss the following questions in a small group.

1 Many of Catherine's strongest friendships are long-distance ones. Do you have any successful long-distance friendships? How often do you communicate with each other? Have the friendships changed at all?

2 Catherine believes that it is OK for friends to disagree with each other and to get angry with each other. In her view, this shows that they care about each other. What do you think? Is it acceptable in your culture for friends who care for each other to express anger openly?

3 Catherine has both male and female friends. Do you have close friends of the opposite sex? If so, how are those friendships different from your same-sex friendships? Are different-sex friendships common in your culture?

3 IN YOUR OWN VOICE

In this section you will conduct a survey on some aspect of friendship, and you will give a presentation about a good friend.

Conducting a survey

Work alone or with a partner.

1➤ Think of a question about friendship that interests you. It might be *How many close friends do you have?* or *What is the most important quality in a friend?*

2➤ Survey 25 or more people. You can include people in and outside of your class. Record their answers along with their gender, nationality, approximate age, and marital status.

3➤ Analyze your data. Add up people's responses and see if there are different trends among people of different genders, ages, and so on. Express your results in percentages and give a brief report to your class.

> *Of the females surveyed, 65% said that what they most wanted in a friend was a "good listener."*

Giving an oral presentation

1➤ Prepare a short oral presentation (four to six minutes) about one of your best friends. Think about when and how you met your friend, why you became friends, and how you maintain your friendship. Write notes and practice speaking from them. Do not memorize your presentation. If possible, get a photo of your friend to show to the class.

2➤ Make your presentation to your class. Try to make your classmates understand why this friend is special to you.

4   ACADEMIC LISTENING AND NOTE TAKING:
Looking at friendship

In this section you will hear and take notes on a two-part lecture given by Ed Rankin, a psychotherapist who works with individuals, couples, and families. The title of the lecture is *Looking at Friendship*. Mr. Rankin will talk about what friendship means to him as an individual and as a psychotherapist, and about male/female differences in friendship.

BEFORE THE LECTURE

Building background knowledge on the topic: Culture notes

1► Read the following paragraph and answer the questions with a partner.

> In his lecture Mr. Rankin will refer to a popular song from the 1960s performed by the American singer and actress Barbra Streisand. The song is "People." Some of the lyrics are: "People who need people are the luckiest people in the world. We're children, needing other children, and yet letting our grown-up pride hide all the need inside."

1 Have you ever heard the song "People"?

2 Do you agree with the writer of the song that it is good to need other people?

3 Explain the lyrics in your own words.

4 What do you think this popular song might have to do with the topic of friendship for a psychotherapist?

2► Mr. Rankin will also bring up a recent U.S. political event in his lecture to illustrate differences between males' and females' friendships. Read the following excerpt and answer the questions as a class.

> Justice Clarence Thomas was nominated to the U.S. Supreme Court by President George Bush in July 1991. In early October, Anita Hill, a professor of law at the University of Oklahoma, testified against Thomas before the Senate Judiciary Committee, which had already recommended that the Senate confirm his appointment. She charged that Thomas had sexually harassed her when they had worked together during the 1980s. The hearings were televised, and millions of Americans watched her testimony. The committee, however, did not change its recommendation for approval, and Thomas's appointment to the Supreme Court was narrowly confirmed by a vote of 52 to 48.

1 What is Clarence Thomas's position?

2 Who testified at Thomas's hearing, and what did she say?

3 How did the public find out what was said at the hearings?

🎧 *Note taking: Using morphology, context, and nonverbal cues to guess word meaning*

W hat should you do when a lecturer uses a term that you do not know? If it seems important, write it down. You can look it up in a dictionary or ask a classmate what it means after class. In the meantime, you may be able to use *morphology*, *spoken context*, and/or *nonverbal cues* to get at least a partial sense of its meaning.

Morphology Using morphology means dividing a word up and looking for parts that you already know. If the lecturer uses a word like *indivisibili-ty*, don't panic! You know that *in-* means *not*, and *-ibility* is related to *ability*, or something being possible. *Divisi-* might remind you of other words in the same family, such as *division* and *divide*. So you see, you have enough information to figure out what *indivisibility* means.

Spoken context As with written context, spoken context will frequently help you with examples, definitions, or paraphrases of the unfamiliar vocabulary. Most lecturers repeat and explain themselves, especially when they are making an important point.

Nonverbal cues Nonverbal cues can give you at least a partial sense of an unfamiliar term. If a speaker stretches out her arms when using the word *gigantic*, for example, you can easily guess that it means *very big*. Or the lecturer may use a particular tone of voice to underscore a word or phrase.

As you listen to a lecture, a partial understanding of an unfamiliar term will often be enough for your purposes. Remember, it is the whole of the lecture that you need to understand, not each of the individual words.

1 ➤ The following terms are used in the lecture. Try to find morphological clues to their meanings.

1 subjective: _____

2 social network, or support systems: _____

3 loners: _____

4 vulnerable: _____

5 incredulous: _____

2 ➤ Now listen to the lecture excerpts. As you listen, spoken context and nonverbal cues will give you more information about the meanings of these terms. Write down what you think each term means. 📼

3 ➤ Compare notes with a partner and then as a class. Explain how you arrived at your answers.

LECTURE, Part One: The role of friendship in psychotherapy

Guessing vocabulary from context

1➤ The following items contain some important vocabulary from Part One of the lecture. Each of the terms is printed in **boldface** and shown in the context in which you will hear it. Work with a partner. Using context, take turns trying to guess the meanings.

_____ *1* Friendship seems like a very **straightforward** topic.

_____ *2* My first memory of consciously **contemplating** friendship was as a young boy.

_____ *3* Is it OK to need people? More and more I tend to answer that question **in the affirmative**.

_____ *4* when I work with a client who's **suicidal**

_____ *5* Suicide is very often the **manifestation** of an abject sense of alienation.

_____ *6* an **abject** sense of alienation

_____ *7* important to **hook them up with** their support systems so that they can be monitored

_____ *8* so that they can be **monitored** and kept safe

_____ *9* adults who consider themselves loners and say they are **content** with that

_____ *10* My sense is that it's almost always the function of a **defense mechanism**.

_____ *11* There can be a lot of pain involved with friendship; it's a **risky business**.

_____ *12* a painful childhood memory of being **cast aside** by one friend

2➤ Match the terms in Step 1 with their definitions by writing the letters in the blanks. Note that the definitions reflect the way the terms are used in the lecture; some of these terms can have different meanings in other contexts.

a way to protect oneself, psychologically
b happy; satisfied
c simple; easy
d thinking about killing oneself
e rejected; forgotten
f thinking about
g miserable; very bad
h sign; demonstration
i connect them with; put them in contact with
j watched closely; observed frequently
k something that may involve danger
l yes

🎧 Listening for specific information

1➤ Read over the following questions on Part One of the lecture. Think about what kind of information you will need in order to answer them.

   1 What first started the lecturer thinking about the importance of friendship? Explain.

   2 Why is the lecturer so concerned with his clients' social networks?

   3 When a client is considering suicide, what are the two reasons why Mr. Rankin looks into the client's support system?

   4 Why is friendship risky?

   5 Why do some people become loners?

2➤ Now listen to Part One of the lecture. Take notes on your own paper. Use the questions in Step 1 as a guide to help you listen for the important points. 📼

Why do some people become loners?

3➤ Use your notes to answer the questions in Step 1. You may write your answers or answer orally with a partner. Answer as fully as you can.

LECTURE, Part Two: How male and female friendships differ

Guessing vocabulary from context

1➤ The following items contain some important vocabulary from Part Two of the lecture. Work with a partner. Using context, take turns trying to guess the meanings.

  _____ *1* Men usually want to arrive at solutions: How can this problem be **fixed**?

  _____ *2* "Why can't she be like my **buddies**?"

  _____ *3* You would have seen this gender difference **played out** in an extraordinary fashion.

  _____ *4* played out in an extraordinary **fashion**

  _____ *5* And I thought: That's **it in a nutshell**.

  _____ *6* They couldn't **fathom** that one friend would not give another friend advice.

2➤ Match the vocabulary terms in Step 1 with their definitions by writing the letters in the blanks.

a a brief and clear picture or example
b solved
c way; manner

d friends (informal)
e believe to be possible
f acted out; demonstrated in a full way

🎧 Listening for specific information

1➤ Read over the following questions on Part Two of the lecture. Think about what kind of information you will need in order to answer them.

1. How do men and women differ in what they enjoy doing together?
2. How do they differ in what they want from each other in a relationship?
3. Retell briefly the story the lecturer told about Anita Hill and Clarence Thomas.
4. How does this story illustrate the point in Question 2?
5. What do we all need from our friends, according to the lecturer?

2➤ Now listen to Part Two of the lecture. Take notes on your own paper. Use the questions in Step 1 as a guide to help you listen for the important points. 📼

3➤ Use your notes to answer the questions in Step 1. You may write your answers or answer orally with a partner. Answer as fully as you can.

AFTER THE LECTURE

Sharing your personal perspective

Discuss the following questions with one or two classmates.

1. The lecturer says that rejection by friends is especially painful for children. Why do you think this is so? Do you remember ever feeling left out or cast aside by friends when you were a child? Do you remember any children who didn't have friends?

2. The lecturer makes some generalizations about male and female friendships. Do you know any people who are exceptions to these generalizations – for example, men who like to talk about how they feel, or women who like to "fix" their friends' problems?

When your friends come to you with their problems, what do you do?

3. What kind of friend are you? When your friends tell you their problems, do you simply listen, or do you try to solve their problems?

4. Were there any points in the lecture that you did not understand or did not agree with? If so, discuss them together.

Considering related information

1► Read the following excerpt about male friendship.

> Ken Hardy, professor of family therapy at Syracuse University, acknowledges that most men . . . usually do require what he calls "the third thing" – basketball or car repair or even intellectual discourse – to justify their togetherness. Nonetheless, he believes that many men derive a certain sense of belonging through their shared pleasure in the activity. . . . Moreover, observes Scott Ailes, a family therapist . . . , "Men can sit around a campfire in silence and honestly feel, 'Boy, this is really great.' I think much of this comes from our histories with our fathers, where we may not have gotten a lot of touching so we felt close when he did things with us. Now, when a man does something for us or with us, that sense of closeness and comfort returns."

2► Answer the following questions in a small group.

1 What does the excerpt say about male friendships in the United States? What does Ken Hardy mean by "the third thing"?

2 Does the information in the excerpt support what the lecturer said about male friendships?

3 Are friendships between men in your culture similar to those described in the excerpt? If so, what "third things" do men in your culture like to do?

4 Do you agree that a boy's relationship with his father strongly influences his male friendships? If so, in what ways?

CHAPTER 10

Love

---

1   GETTING STARTED

In this section you will read and talk about what makes two people fall in love, and what makes love last, and you will play matchmaker for six single people.

Reading and thinking about the topic

1➤ Read the following passage.

> What makes two people fall in love? What makes love last? These are two very different questions. It is often said that "opposites attract," and in some respects this is true. A lot of couples have certain personality differences that complement one another. For example, he might be shy and she might be outgoing. However, research shows that love relationships are more likely to last if two people "match" each other – that is, if they have similar backgrounds, values, opinions, and interests. This makes good sense, if we think about it. Two people with similar backgrounds are more likely to understand each other and to agree on the wide range of issues that we face in long-term relationships – everything from how to raise children to what kind of car to buy.

2➤ Answer the following questions according to the information in the passage.

1 How would you answer the two questions at the beginning of this passage?

2 What is one way in which two people might complement each other?

3 In what ways do most successful couples match, according to research?

3▶ Discuss your own experiences and opinions with a partner.

1 Think of a married couple that you know – for example, your parents. In what ways are they similar to each other?

2 In what ways are the same two people different? Do you think these differences have a positive or negative effect on the relationship?

Personalizing the topic

1▶ Work alone. Imagine that you have gone to a matchmaker who will help you to find a mate. Think about what kind of person you are and what kind of mate you want.

2▶ Check (✓) all the characteristics that apply to you. Add another term that applies to you in each blank.

I am . . .		*I enjoy . . .*	
❑ shy	❑ sensitive	❑ pop music	❑ going to movies
❑ serious	❑ mature	❑ jazz	❑ art
❑ outgoing	❑ responsible	❑ classical music	❑ camping
❑ athletic	❑ easygoing	❑ playing sports	❑ hiking
❑ fun-loving	❑ _____	❑ watching sports	❑ shopping
❑ adventurous	❑ _____	❑ reading	❑ _____
❑ hard-working	❑ _____	❑ cooking	❑ _____

3▶ Now think about what characteristics you are looking for in a mate. Check all the terms that apply. Add another term in each blank.

I'd like someone who is . . .		*I'd like someone who enjoys . . .*	
❑ shy	❑ sensitive	❑ pop music	❑ going to movies
❑ serious	❑ mature	❑ jazz	❑ art
❑ outgoing	❑ responsible	❑ classical music	❑ camping
❑ athletic	❑ easygoing	❑ playing sports	❑ hiking
❑ fun-loving	❑ _____	❑ watching sports	❑ shopping
❑ adventurous	❑ _____	❑ reading	❑ _____
❑ hard-working	❑ _____	❑ cooking	❑ _____

4▶ Compare the qualities you checked for yourself with those you checked for a mate. Are you looking for someone who *matches* you or someone who *complements* you?

🎧 Listening for details

> **S**ometimes you cannot tell while you are listening to a speaker which are the important details and which are the unimportant ones, so you must try to take notes on as many details as possible.

1➤ Listen to the tape. You will hear six people who are looking for a mate give a brief description of themselves. Take notes as you listen. Write down as many details as you can. 📼

    1 Les: _____

    _____

    2 Michael: _____

    _____

    3 Alicia: _____

    _____

    4 Frank: _____

    _____

    5 Sara: _____

    _____

    6 Suzanne: _____

    _____

2➤ Compare notes with a partner. Did you write the same information?

3➤ Play matchmaker. Decide which person would be happiest with whom. Discuss your reasons with your partner.

4➤ As a class, compare your matches. Which matches do you think would be successful, and why?

*"We have a lot in common.
We're both insanely greedy!"*

2 AMERICAN VOICES: Ann and Jim

In this section you will hear a married couple, Ann and Jim, talk about how they met and why their relationship is successful.

BEFORE THE INTERVIEW

Sharing your cultural perspective

1► Work with a partner from another culture if possible. Ask questions about marriage in your partner's culture. If you are from the same culture, answer the questions together.

My partner's culture/country: _____

 1 At about what age do couples meet each other? _____
 2 Where and how do couples meet? _____ .
 3 How long on average do couples wait to get married? _____
 4 Do most couples have children? How many children? _____
 5 What percentage of married couples get divorced? _____

2► Discuss with your partner whether any of the information above has changed recently, and, if so, how. For example, are couples getting married earlier than they did in the past?

INTERVIEW WITH ANN AND JIM, Part One: Courtship

> Here are some words and expressions from Part One of the interview, in the context in which you will hear them.
>
> *How did you **initially** get interested in each other?:* at first; in the beginning
> *attending the same little **country** church:* in a rural area; not in or near a city
> *I fell **head-over-heels** in love:* very quickly and completely
> *This one **stuck**:* lasted; didn't disappear
> *before he actually **proposed**:* asked, "Will you marry me?"
> *I was so **relieved**:* happy after a period of worrying
> *Did Jim **give you any encouragement**?:* show an interest; seem to be attracted
> *I wasn't very good at **showing** [my interest]:* communicating
> *doing my **internship**:* period of supervised work in a hospital at the end of medical school training
> ***the Peace Corps**:* an organization that sends volunteers to work in developing countries
> *a rather **oblique** proposal:* indirect
> *permission **to have Ann's hand**:* to marry [Ann]
> ***It was worth the wait.**:* I am glad that I waited.
> *I feel very **fortunate**:* lucky

🎧 *Listening for specific information*

1▸ Read the following questions before you listen to Part One of the interview.

Ann and Jim

  1 How long have Ann and Jim been married?

  2 How old were they when they first met?

  3 What was Ann's first impression of Jim?

  4 What was Ann worried about at first?

  5 How many years was it before Jim proposed?

  6 Why and how did Jim finally propose?

  7 Why does Ann feel "very fortunate"?

2▸ Now listen to Part One of the interview. Write short answers to the questions. ▭

3▸ Compare answers with a partner.

INTERVIEW WITH ANN AND JIM, Part Two: Making marriage work

> Here are some words and expressions from Part Two of the interview.
>
> *It wasn't a **one-sided** kind of thing:* where one person is much stronger or more important
>
> *Our **faith** is very important to us:* religious beliefs
>
> *differences that **work to** your **advantage**:* help; benefit
>
> *Ann is very **meticulous**:* careful and exact; neat
>
> *a **phenomenal** record of our 30 years together:* amazing; surprising; wonderful
>
> *They're all **catalogued** neatly **in albums**:* filed in books designed to hold photographs
>
> *Jim has **alluded to** it:* mentioned indirectly
>
> *We**'re committed to** our marriage:* want to make successful; promise to support
>
> *experiences that have **bonded** you:* united; brought closer together emotionally
>
> ***not necessarily the happiest of times**:* unhappy times (expressed indirectly to be polite)
>
> *They were **challenging** [years]:* difficult, but in a positive way

🎧 Listening for specific information

1➤ Read the following questions before you listen to Part Two of the interview.

1. What does Jim mean when he says that his and Ann's relationship isn't one-sided?
2. What interests and beliefs do Ann and Jim share?
3. Jim talks about a difference between himself and Ann. What is it?
4. What quality do both Ann and Jim mention as important to the success of their marriage?
5. Describe the experiences that have "bonded" Ann and Jim. Were they good or bad? Explain.

2➤ Now listen to Part Two of the interview. Write short answers to the questions. 📼

3➤ Compare answers with a partner and then as a class.

AFTER THE INTERVIEW

Sharing your personal and cultural perspective

Discuss the following questions in a group with classmates of both sexes if possible.

1. Ann says that Jim gave her *very little* encouragement during the eleven years before they got married. Why do you think this was the case?
2. Would it be common for a woman in your culture to wait eleven years to marry the man she loved? Would a man wait that long for a woman?
3. In what ways is the marriage of Ann and Jim different from the typical successful marriage in your culture? In what ways is it similar?
4. What experiences do you think bond a couple? Name as many as you can.

Ann in the Peace Corps in Ethiopia

Considering related information

1➤ Here are ten features of personal appearance that people might notice when they first meet someone. Try to predict whether men or women would be more likely to notice each feature in someone of the opposite sex. Write *M* next to features that you think men would notice, and write *W* next to those that you think women would notice.

____ clothing   ____ figure/body   ____ smile   ____ teeth   ____ hands
____ eyes   ____ face   ____ hair   ____ height   ____ legs

2➤ The following information was taken from a study that asked men and women: "When you meet someone of the opposite sex, which one or two things about physical appearance do you tend to notice first?" One of you should look *only* at Table A, and the other *only* at Table B. Ask your partner questions to fill in the blanks in your table.

Table A

Percent of Males	Percent of Females	Who first notice:
29	___	clothing
___	30	eyes
45	___	figure/body
___	27	face
24	___	smile
___	16	hair
11	___	teeth
___	8	height
1	___	hands
___	<.5	legs

Student A

What percentage of women first notice clothing?

Table B

Percent of Males	Percent of Females	Who first notice:
___	35	clothing
22	___	eyes
___	29	figure/body
34	___	face
___	27	smile
16	___	hair
___	5	teeth
8	___	height
___	2	hands
6	___	legs

Student B

What percentage of men first notice clothing?

3➤ As a class, make comparative statements about men and women in the United States based on information in the boxes.

When first meeting someone of the opposite sex, men are twice as likely as women to notice teeth.

4➤ What do *you* notice first? Take a survey in your class and compile the results on the board. Do male and female students answer differently?

3   IN YOUR OWN VOICE

In this section you will survey your classmates on a topic related to love, and you will interview a married couple.

Conducting a survey

Do the following activity alone or with a partner.

1➤ Think of a topic related to love or marriage that interests you. Some possible topics are: love marriages versus arranged marriages, the importance of personality versus physical appearance, and matching versus complementing. Look back at *Personalizing the topic* in Section 1 and *Sharing your cultural perspective* in Section 2 for more ideas.

2➤ Write three or four questions about your topic. (See *Conducting a survey* in Chapter 2, Section 3 [page 23] for question guidelines.)

3➤ Survey twenty or more people. You can include people in and outside of your class. Record their answers along with their gender, nationality, approximate age, and marital status.

4➤ Analyze your data. Add up people's responses and look for different trends among people of different genders, nationalities, and so on. Express your results in percentages and give a brief report to your class.

Gathering data

1➤ Get ready to interview a married couple about their relationship. Choose a couple outside of your class and prepare your questions first. You can use the same kinds of questions that you heard in the interview with Ann and Jim. Think of some questions of your own as well.

> *How did you get interested in each other?*
> *What interests do you share?*
> *How do you complement each other?*

2➤ Interview the couple. Encourage them to tell stories to support their answers. As they talk, take brief notes.

3➤ Give a short report on your interview.

4 ACADEMIC LISTENING AND NOTE TAKING: Love – What's it all about?

In this section you will hear and take notes on a two-part lecture given by Dr. Robert Atkins, a professor of psychology. The title of the lecture is *Love – What's It All About?* Professor Atkins will explore various factors that influence people in their choice of a mate.

BEFORE THE LECTURE

Building background knowledge on the topic

1► You have just read that the lecture will discuss some of the different factors that influence people when they are choosing a mate. Look over the list of factors that Professor Atkins plans to cover in his lecture.

> *Week 9 Lecture: Love – What's it all about?*
> • the matching hypothesis – possible areas of similarity
> • complementarity
> • the Romeo and Juliet effect

2► Discuss the following questions with a partner.

1 What do you think Dr. Atkins means by "the matching hypothesis"?

2 What are some areas of similarity between partners that Dr. Atkins might mention?

3 You have seen the verb *to complement* earlier in this chapter. Explain what it means. What do you think the noun *complementarity* means?

4 Do you know the story of the young lovers Romeo and Juliet, from the play by William Shakespeare? Summarize the story briefly with your partner. How does the story end?

Romeo and Juliet

5 If the "Romeo and Juliet effect" is an explanation for why some people fall in love, what do you think it means?

🎧 Note taking: Taking advantage of rhetorical questions

> **Y**ou will find that many American lecturers like to ask questions of their students as a way to keep them interested. In the United States, students are encouraged to participate and express opinions, sometimes even in a lecture setting. As a foreign student, you may not feel comfortable doing this at first; it may be culturally unfamiliar as well as linguistically challenging. Do not feel that you must speak.
>
> However, you may find that these questions can help you in two ways. First, the lecturer will usually pause after asking them, thus slowing down the pace of the lecture a little bit and giving you time to catch up. Second, these questions are often asked in such a way that you can predict the answers to some extent. In this sense, many are not questions at all but simply a way for the lecturer to get students to demonstrate their understanding of a point. When a lecturer asks, "Do you think that this kind of marriage will succeed?" this may really mean "I am telling you that it will not succeed." Such questions are called *rhetorical questions*.
>
> Rhetorical questions can also give you clues about what is coming next. For example, after giving some specific examples to support a point, a lecturer may look up and ask something like, "Uh, okay, what else?" From this question you can guess that at least one more example or point is coming.

1➤ Listen to six rhetorical questions excerpted from the lecture. After each question, try to predict what the lecturer will say next. Write your prediction. Then, with a partner, recall the questions in your own words and compare your predictions. 📼

1 _____
_____

2 _____
_____

3 _____
_____

4 _____
_____

5 _____
_____

6 _____
_____

2➤ Now listen to the rhetorical questions again. This time, you will hear what follows. Were your predictions mostly correct? 📼

LECTURE, Part One: The matching hypothesis

Guessing vocabulary from context

1➤ The following items contain some important vocabulary from Part One of the lecture. Each of the terms is printed in **boldface** in the context in which it occurs. Work with a partner. Using context, take turns trying to guess the meanings.

_____ 1 The **sociobiology** people would tend to say you fall in love unconsciously.

_____ 2 Guys that are tall and muscular would produce a good **gene pool**.

_____ 3 **homogeneity,** or similarity

_____ 4 Some people call this the **matching hypothesis**, that we tend to be attracted by somebody who is like us.

_____ 5 Maybe she's a **"ten,"** and he's a "three."

_____ 6 if she graduated from graduate school, and he **flunked out of** kindergarten

_____ 7 and he flunked out of **kindergarten**

_____ 8 She was afraid it would **break up** the marriage.

_____ 9 He kept **bugging** her about her being a college graduate.

_____ 10 She didn't want to have even more of a **gap**.

2➤ Match the terms in Step 1 with their definitions by writing the letters in the blanks. Note that the definitions reflect the way in which the terms are used in the lecture; some of these terms can have different meanings in other contexts.

Why do you fall in love with one person – but not another person?

a end; destroy
b distance between two people, opinions, and so on
c failed; did not continue in school
d study of the relationship between nature and society
e extremely attractive (on a scale of one to ten)
f year of preschool, before elementary school
g source of hereditary traits; DNA
h sameness
i theory that similar people make the best mates
j complaining to

🎧 Outlining practice

1➤ Look at the following general outline of Part One of the lecture.

```
                LOVE – WHAT'S IT ALL ABOUT? Part One
   I. the matching hypothesis = _____
      A. possible areas of similarity
      1. physical
         e.g., _____
      2. personality
      3. _____
      4. _____
      5. education
         e.g., _____
      6. same interests
      7. _____
      8. _____
      9. race
     10. age: _____
     11. _____
```

2➤ Now listen to Part One of the lecture. Take notes on your own paper. 📼

3➤ Use your notes to complete the outline. You do not need to include everything; just fill in the blanks in the outline.

4➤ Compare outlines with a partner. Help each other if you did not hear all the areas of similarity mentioned. Remember, your outlines do not have to be exactly the same.

LECTURE, Part Two: The matching hypothesis (continued) and other theories

Guessing vocabulary from context

1➤ The following items contain some important vocabulary from Part Two of the lecture. Work with a partner. Using context, take turns trying to guess the meanings.

_____   *1* But you might say, "He's **Catholic** and she's **Jewish**."

_____   *2* We also want to marry someone who **validates** our ideas.

_____   *3* The idea that opposites attract, that's **complementary** theory.

_____   *4* If a person is **dominant**, is he or she better off with another dominant person?

_____   *5* Is he or she **better off** with another dominant person?

_____   *6* a person that's more **submissive**, who likes people telling him or her what to do

2➤ Match the terms in Step 1 with their definitions by writing the letters in the blanks.

   a controlling; wanting to tell others what to do
   b examples of religious faiths
   c having differences that work together to act as advantages
   d agrees with; confirms
   e obedient; happy to do what he or she is told
   f more likely to be happy or successful

🎧 *Outlining practice*

1➤ Look at the following general outline of Part Two of the lecture.

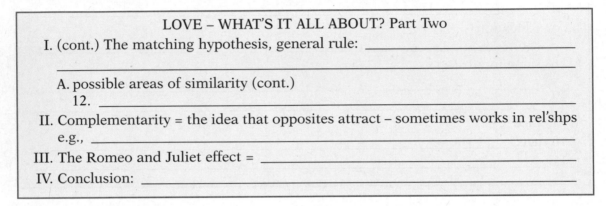

> LOVE – WHAT'S IT ALL ABOUT? Part Two
>
> I. (cont.) The matching hypothesis, general rule: _____
> _____
>
>   A. possible areas of similarity (cont.)
>   12. _____
> II. Complementarity = the idea that opposites attract – sometimes works in rel'shps
>   e.g., _____
> III. The Romeo and Juliet effect = _____
> IV. Conclusion: _____

2➤ Now listen to Part Two of the lecture. Take notes on your own paper. 📼

3➤ Use your notes to complete the outline.

4➤ Compare outlines with a partner. Remember, your outlines do not have to be exactly the same.

"They're a perfect match – she's high-maintenance, and he can fix anything."

AFTER THE LECTURE

Applying general concepts to specific data

Read the following questions and answer them with one or two classmates.

1 Go over the factors mentioned in the lecture. Which of these apply to the relationship between Ann and Jim? Which do not apply, in your opinion? Explain.

2 Look again at the data in the task *Considering related information* in Section 2. How do you think this information relates to what Professor Atkins said in his lecture? How important are first impressions? What purpose do you think they serve?

Sharing your personal and cultural perspective

Read and think about the following questions, and then share your ideas with a small group.

1 The lecturer stated that as a general rule people of the same religion and race have a better chance of staying married. Do you know any couples of mixed race, religion, or culture? Do you think that they face more difficulties than other couples?

2 How powerful do you think the "Romeo and Juliet effect" is? Do you know of any couples who have experienced opposition from their families? What was the result?

3 This chapter has focused on marriages in the United States and what makes them successful. It's important to remember that in the United States, about 50 percent of all first marriages end in divorce. Considering the information that you heard in the lecture, why do you think there are so many failed marriages in the United States?

4 Were there any points in the lecture that you did not understand or did not agree with? Ask your classmates about them, or ask your teacher.

Credits

TEXT

Pages 5 and 9: Adapted from the brochure "Stress in College: What Everyone Should Know." Copyright © 1996, with permission from American College Health Association.

Page 9: Entry on conditioning adapted from *The Oxford Companion to the Mind,* edited by Richard L. Gregory, Oxford University Press (1987), by permission of Oxford University Press.

Page 14: Summarized from *The University of California Berkeley Wellness Newsletter,* October 1993.

Page 38: Statistics from "What Grown-Ups Don't Understand," *The New York Times Magazine,* October 8, 1995, p. 81. Copyright © 1995 by The New York Times Company. Reprinted by permission.

Page 45: Poll results from "Growing Up Fast and Frightened," *Newsweek,* November 22, 1993, p. 53. ©1993 Newsweek, Inc. All rights reserved. Reprinted by permission.

Page 53: Paragraph adapted from *Psychology: Being Human, Fourth Edition* by Zick Rubin and Elton B. McNeil, HarperCollins Publishers, 1985, p. 213. Reprinted with permission.

Page 58: Family statistics from *The 1997 Information Please Almanac.*

Page 66: Charts from *Wechsler's Measurement and Appraisal of Adult Intelligence, Fifth Edition,* by Joseph D. Matarazzo, p. 296. Copyright © 1972 by Oxford University Press, Inc. Used by permission of Oxford University Press, Inc.

Page 77: Excerpt from "Group Seeks to Alter S.A.T.'s to Raise the Scores of Girls" by Katharine Q. Seelye, *The New York Times,* March 14, 1997. Copyright © 1997/95 by The New York Times Company. Reprinted by permission.

Page 84: Excerpt from "For Twins, Double Jackpot on the S.A.T." by Peter Applebome, *The New York Times,* November 10, 1995. Copyright © 1997/95 by The New York Times Company. Reprinted by permission.

Pages 92: Charts adapted from *Understanding Body Talk* by Thomas Aylesworth, Franklin Watts, 1979, p. 5.

Page 105: Excerpt from "Encounters" by Stephen Thayer, *Psychology Today*, March 1988, p. 36. Reprinted with permission from *Psychology Today Magazine*, Copyright © 1988 (Sussex Publishers, Inc.).

Page 124: Excerpt from "The Gift of Friendship" by Marian Sandmaier, *The Family Therapy Networker*, July/August 1995, p. 32. This article first appeared in *The Family Therapy Networker* and is excerpted with permission.

Page 132: Chart adapted from a survey by Roper Starch Worldwide (Report 83-5) reported in *Public Opinion* (vol. 6, no. 4), August/September 1993. Reprinted with permission.

CARTOONS

Page 17: Gary Larson, "Primitive Peer Pressure," The Farside © FarWorks, Inc. Used by permission of Universal Press Syndicate. All Rights Reserved.

Page 57: Tom Cheney © 1995 from The New Yorker Collection. All Rights Reserved.

Page 63: Gary Larson, "Primitive Spelling Bee," The Farside © FarWorks, Inc. Used by permission of Universal Press Syndicate. All Rights Reserved.

Page 78: Gary Larson, "Midvale School for Gifted," The Farside © FarWorks, Inc. Used by permission of Universal Press Syndicate. All Rights Reserved.

Page 128: Joseph Farris © 1998 from The New Yorker Collection. All Rights Reserved.

Page 138: Edward Koren © 1996 from The New Yorker Collection. All Rights Reserved.

ILLUSTRATIONS

Page 22: Smoking Graph: A Giant Habit, *The New York Times*, March 16, 1996. Copyright © 1996 by The New York Times Company.

Page 27, 33, 61, 78, 87, 99, 136: Randy Jones

Page 16, 79: Suffolk Technical Illustrators

PHOTOGRAPHS

Cover: © Christie's Images, London/Abstrakter Kopf, Jawlensky, Alexej Van/SuperStock

Page 1: © Frank Cezus/Tony Stone Images

Page 2: © Bruce Ayres/Tony Stone Images

Page 3: © Roy Morsch/The Stock Market

Task Index

Page numbers in boldface indicate tasks that are headed by commentary boxes.